INES DE LA FRESSANGE
PARIS

Parisian Chic City Guide

ENGLISH EDITION

Editorial Director: Kate Mascaro
Editor: Helen Adedotun
Design: Noémie Levain
Translation from the French: Elizabeth Heard
Copyediting: Lindsay Porter
Typesetting: Claude-Olivier Four
Photo Research: Kate Reiners
Color Separation: Bussière, Paris

Printed in Slovakia by TBB

Simultaneously published in French as *Mon Paris*

87, quai Panhard et Levassor
75647 Paris Cedex 13
editions.flammarion.com

15 16 17 3 2 1

ISBN: 978-2-08-020236-9

Legal Deposit: 10/2015

Publisher's note: The maps of Paris reproduced in this book are from the Taride archives and date from 1971. We warmly thank Géraldine Boulanger and her team for their collaboration.

Parisian Chic City Guide

Ines de la Fressange

with Sophie Gachet

Flammarion

LEVALLOIS-PERRET
Porte de Clichy
St-Ouen
Guy Môquet
Jules Joffrin
Lamarck Caulaincourt
Brochant
CIMETIÈRE MONTMARTRE
LA FOURCHE
Abbesses
SACRÉ CŒUR
PIGALLE
Anvers
Blanche
PL. DE CLICHY
RER
BERTHIER
PEREIRE
BOULEVARD
Porte de Champerret
MAIRIE DU XVII ARR.
Rome
Liège
ÉGLISE DE LA TRINITÉ
St-Georges
N.-D. DE LORETTE
Trinité
Wagram
Malesherbes
VILLIERS
Europe
ST-LAZARE
N.D. de Lorette
Le Peletier
RICHELIEU DROUOT
Courcelles
Monceau
PARC MONCEAU
Ternes
ST-AUGUSTIN
St-Augustin
HAVRE-CAUMARTIN
CH. D'ANTIN
Quatre Septembre
AUBER
OPÉRA
R.E.R.
AVENUE FRIEDLAND
MIROMESNIL
MADELEINE
Bourse
Argentine
ARC DE TRIOMPHE
CH. DE GAULLE-ÉTOILE
George V
St-Philippe du Roule
ÉGL. DE LA MADELEINE
BIBLIOTHÈQUE NATIONALE
BANQUE DE FRANCE
Pyramides
Kléber
FRANKLIN D. ROOSEVELT
CH. ÉLYSÉES-CLEMENCEAU
CONCORDE
PALAIS ROYAL
LES HALLES
FORUM DES HALLES
GRAND PALAIS
PETIT PALAIS
Tuileries
JARDIN DES TUILERIES
ORANGERIE
Iéna
ALMA-MARCEAU
COURS ALBERT 1er
COURS LA REINE
Louvre
Q. des Tuileries
MUSÉE D'ORSAY
PONT DE L'ALMA
INVALIDES
Ch. des Députés
PALAIS BOURBON
Pont-Neuf
SOLFÉRINO
CHÂTELET
PALAIS DE JUSTICE
TOUR EIFFEL
La Tour-Maubourg
ÉCOLE DES BEAUX-ARTS
INSTITUT DE FRANCE
École Militaire
Varenne
Bac
St-Germain-des-Prés
Mabillon
ST MICHEL
FONTAINE ST-MICHEL
ODÉON
SÈVRES-BABYLONE
St-Sulpice
St-François-Xavier
Rennes
CASERNE DUPLEIX
LA SORBONNE
MUSÉE DE CLUNY
COLLÈGE DE FRANCE
Dupleix
LA MOTTE-PICQUET-GRENELLE
Cambronne
Ségur
Vaneau
DUROC
St-Placide
Émile Zola
Sèvres-Lecourbe
Falguière
PALAIS DU LUXEMBOURG
Commerce
MONTPARNASSE-BIENVENÜE
TOUR MAINE MONTPARNASSE
N. Dame-des-Champs
Luxembourg
JARDIN DU LUXEMBOURG
PANTHÉON
Volontaires
PASTEUR
Vaugirard
ÉGLISE ST-LAMBERT
GARE MONTPARNASSE
Vavin
Edgar Quinet
Convention
INSTITUT PASTEUR
Gaîté
RASPAIL
Port-Royal
BOUL DE PORT
OBSERVATOIRE
HÔPITAL COCHIN
Porte de Versailles
PARC DES EXPOSITIONS
PARC GEORGES BRASSENS
N.D. DU TRAVAIL
Pernety
DENFERT-ROCHEREAU
Plaisance
BOULEVARD
PRISON DE LA SANTÉ
ST-JACQUES
St-Jacques
Glacière
HÔPITAL BROUSSAIS
Porte de Vanves
Mouton-Duvernet
CENTRE PSYCHIATRIQUE STE-ANNE
LEFEBVRE
Alésia
BOULEVARD
BRUNE
PORTE D'ORLÉANS
RÉSERVOIRS DE LA VANNE
Malakoff-Plateau de Vanves

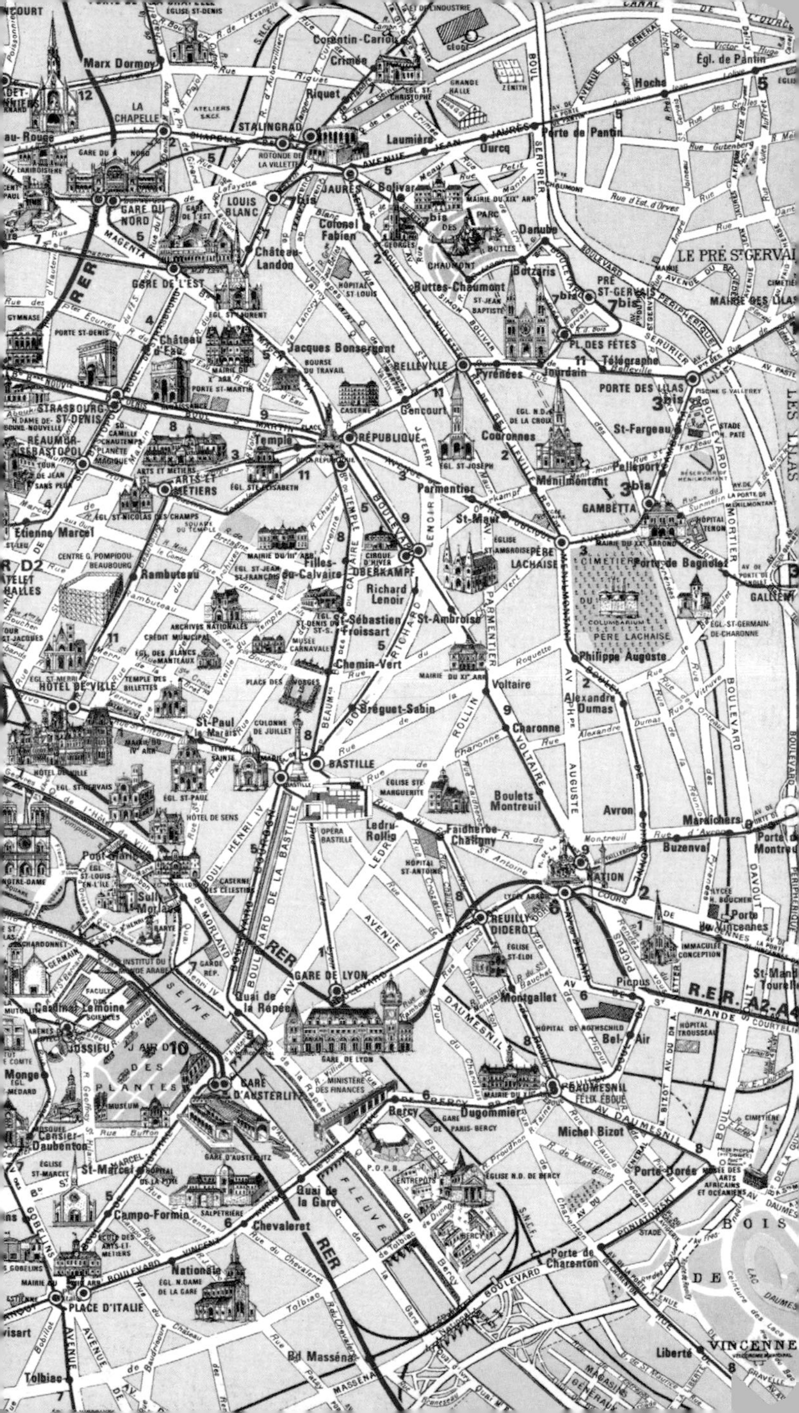

Marx Dormoy
LA CHAPELLE
GARE DU NORD
GARE DE L'EST
STALINGRAD
ROTONDE DE LA VILLETTE
Corentin-Cariou
Crimée
Riquet
Laumière
Ourcq
Porte de Pantin
Hoche
Égl. de Pantin
ZENITH
GRANDE HALLE
ATELIERS S.N.C.F.
JAURÈS
LOUIS BLANC
Colonel Fabien
Château-Landon
Bolivar
MAIRIE DU XIXe ARR^T
Danube
Botzaris
Buttes-Chaumont
PRÉ ST-GERVAIS
LE PRÉ S^T GERVAIS
MAIRIE DES LILAS
PL. DES FÊTES
Télégraphe
Jourdain
Pyrénées
BELLEVILLE
PORTE DES LILAS
St-Fargeau
Pelleport
GAMBETTA
Ménilmontant
Couronnes
Goncourt
RÉPUBLIQUE
Temple
Jacques Bonsergent
Château d'Eau
PORTE ST-DENIS
PORTE ST-MARTIN
STRASBOURG-ST-DENIS
RÉAUMUR-SÉBASTOPOL
ARTS ET MÉTIERS
Étienne Marcel
CENTRE G. POMPIDOU-BEAUBOURG
Rambuteau
Parmentier
St-Maur
PÈRE LACHAISE
CIMETIÈRE DU PÈRE LACHAISE
Porte de Bagnolet
GALLIENI
Filles-du-Calvaire
OBERKAMPF
Richard Lenoir
St-Sébastien Froissart
St-Ambroise
Chemin-Vert
Bréguet-Sabin
Voltaire
Philippe Auguste
Alexandre Dumas
Charonne
HÔTEL DE VILLE
St-Paul
BASTILLE
OPÉRA BASTILLE
Ledru-Rollin
Faidherbe-Chaligny
Boulets Montreuil
Avron
Maraîchers
Buzenval
Porte de Montreuil
NATION
REUILLY DIDEROT
Porte de Vincennes
Pont-Marie
Sully Morland
Quai de la Rapée
GARE DE LYON
Montgallet
Picpus
Bel-Air
DAUMESNIL
Michel Bizot
Porte Dorée
Cardinal Lemoine
JUSSIEU
Monge
Censier-Daubenton
St-Marcel
Campo-Formio
GARE D'AUSTERLITZ
Quai de la Gare
Chevaleret
Nationale
PLACE D'ITALIE
Tolbiac
Bercy
Dugommier
Porte de Charenton
Liberté
Bd Masséna
SEINE
FLEUVE
JARDIN DES PLANTES
BOIS DE VINCENNES
R.E.R. A2-A4
RER

"I'm looking for a good restaurant near Saint-Germain-des-Prés; any suggestions?"

"I just moved and I need to buy some furniture—where should I go?"

"I'm looking for a dress and I want a store where I can't go wrong. Help!"

For years, I've been receiving text messages from friends with requests like these. I told them all about Google, but apparently, it's no match for me! I published *Parisian Chic* in 2011, which included some of my favorite addresses, and that satisfied them for a little while.
But soon enough they were clamoring for more.
Which prompted me to write this city guide, full of all the new places I've discovered since then. I'll be thrilled if it helps you out, too.

Vive Paris!

Ines

Ier & IIe ARRONDISSEMENTS

The Heart of Paris

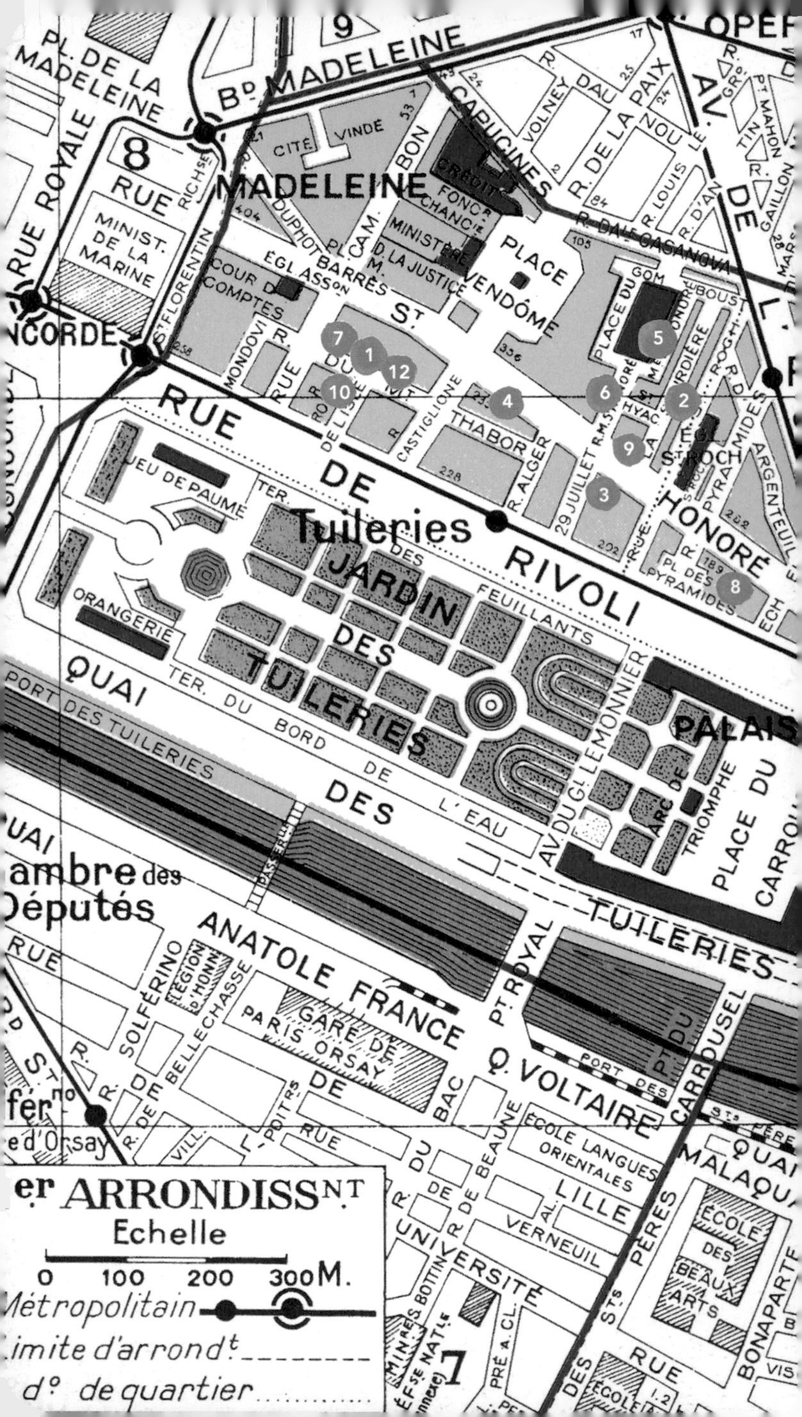
BD MADELEINE
PL. DE LA MADELEINE
RUE ROYALE
MADELEINE
MINIST. DE LA MARINE
COUR DES COMPTES
PLACE VENDÔME
RUE DE RIVOLI
Tuileries
JARDIN DES TUILERIES
JEU DE PAUME
ORANGERIE
TER. DES FEUILLANTS
TER. DU BORD DE L'EAU
QUAI DES TUILERIES
PORT DES TUILERIES
AV. DU GL LEMONNIER
ARC DE TRIOMPHE
PLACE DU CARROUSEL
PALAIS
ST HONORÉ
ST ROCH
R. DE CASTIGLIONE
R. DU MONT THABOR
R. D'ALGER
R. DU 29 JUILLET
R. DE LA PAIX
AV. DE L'OPÉRA
PL. DES PYRAMIDES
CAPUCINES
Chambre des Députés
QUAI ANATOLE FRANCE
GARE DE PARIS ORSAY
PT ROYAL
Q. VOLTAIRE
PT DU CARROUSEL
QUAI MALAQUAIS
ÉCOLE LANGUES ORIENTALES
ÉCOLE DES BEAUX ARTS
RUE DU BAC
RUE DE LILLE
R. DE VERNEUIL
R. DE L'UNIVERSITÉ
R. DE BEAUNE
RUE DES STS PÈRES
R. DE BELLECHASSE
SOLFÉRINO
LÉGION D'HONN
1er ARRONDISSNT
Echelle
0 100 200 300 M.
Métropolitain
Limite d'arrondt
do de quartier

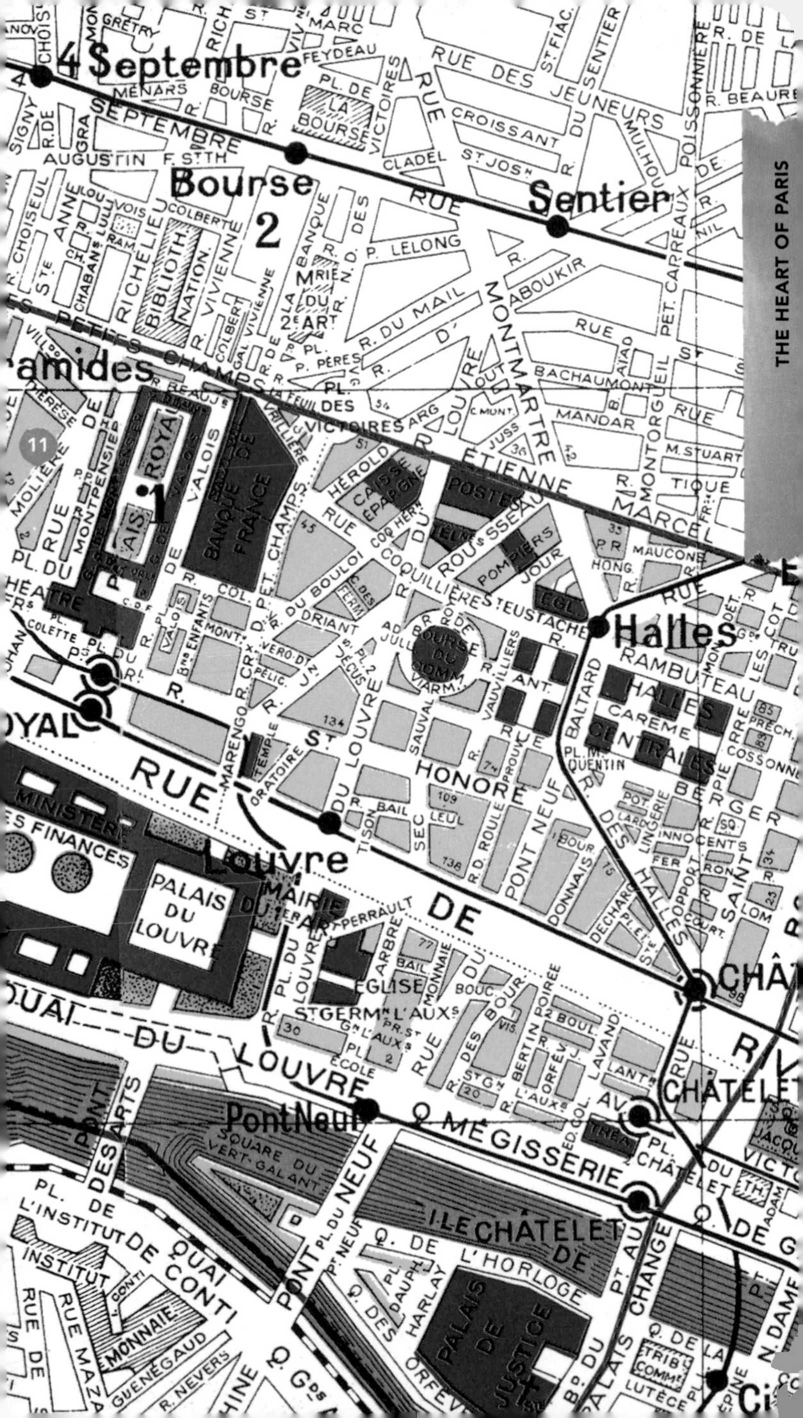
4 Septembre
Bourse
2
Sentier
amides
1
Halles
Louvre
Pont Neuf
RUE DES JEUNEURS
R. CROISSANT
RUE DU SENTIER
LA BOURSE
BIBLIOTH. NATION.
R. RICHELIEU
R. VIVIENNE
R. DU MAIL
R. ABOUKIR
R. MONTMARTRE
RUE BACHAUMONT
R. MANDAR
R. MONTORGUEIL
PL. DES VICTOIRES
R. ÉTIENNE MARCEL
BANQUE DE FRANCE
PALAIS ROYAL
R. DE VALOIS
RUE MONTPENSIER
RUE MOLIÈRE
CAISSE ÉPARGNE
POSTES
POMPIERS
R. COQUILLIÈRE
R. DU BOULOI
BOURSE DU COMM.
St EUSTACHE
R. RAMBUTEAU
HALLES CENTRALES
R. BALTARD
RUE ST HONORÉ
RUE DE RIVOLI
MINISTÈRE DES FINANCES
PALAIS DU LOUVRE
MAIRIE DU 1er ARt
ÉGLISE St GERMAIN L'AUXs
R. DU PONT NEUF
QUAI DU LOUVRE
Q. MÉGISSERIE
CHÂTELET
SQUARE DU VERT GALANT
PONT DES ARTS
PONT NEUF
PL. DE L'INSTITUT
QUAI DE CONTI
INSTITUT
MONNAIE
R. GUÉNÉGAUD
R. NEVERS
Q. DE L'HORLOGE
PALAIS DE JUSTICE
PT. AU CHANGE
BD. DU PALAIS
TRIB. COMMl
N. DAME
R. DES HALLES
R. DES LOMBARDS
RUE BERGER
R. DE LA FERRONNERIE
R. SAINT DENIS

Stouls

36, rue du Mont-Thabor, Ier
Tel. +33 (0)1 42 60 29 97 — www.stouls.net

Why go? This is the place to go if you want an article of leather or suede clothing that fits like a second skin and is as soft as cashmere. Breaking all the rules for this material, designer Aurelia Stouls started with leather t-shirts. Sexy, chic, and—more importantly—practical: Stouls leathers are machine-washable like denim.

The must-have Difficult to choose only one, because all Stouls creations are flattering. I love the flared napa lambskin trousers that are very 1970. She makes them every season; I bought the Starsky model.

Say it like La Parisienne

"Even my sweatpants come from Stouls!"

laContrie

11, rue de la Sourdière, Ier
Tel. +33 (0)1 49 27 06 44 — www.lacontrie.com

Why go? If you like to be unique, you have to stop here to order a personalized bag. Choose your leather, zippers, and all the finishing details; you can even customize the handle straps.

The must-have The Saint-Roch bag, a timeless gem. You'll never tire of it. And it gets more and more beautiful over time.

Say it like La Parisienne
"My dog loves his laContrie collar!"

Colette

213, rue Saint-Honoré, Ier
Tel. +33 (0)1 55 35 33 90 — www.colette.fr

Why go? This boutique has become a pilgrimage destination on a par with the Eiffel Tower. Nothing's been left unsaid about the legendary Colette, but here's what you need to remember: it's impossible to be out of style when sporting an outfit or accessory from Colette. And if anyone utters a word against your purchase, a simple "I bought it at Colette" will stop the critic in their tracks, knowing they're the one who's out of touch.

The must-have An iPhone case—so you can say "not everything from Colette is expensive." Of course you can also find jewelry from well-known names and clothing that you're sure to have seen in our favorite fashion magazines.

Say it like La Parisienne

"I bought it at Colette, but I first saw it in New York ages ago."

"A LOT OF PEOPLE FORGOT THAT FIFI STARTED HER CAREER SINGING IN EGYPTIAN ARABIC."

Fifi Chachnil

231, rue Saint-Honoré, Ier
Tel. +33 (0)1 42 61 21 83 — www.fifichachnil.com

Why go? Fifi has mastered the art of designing lingerie that is sexy without ever looking trashy. She has her own distinctive style, a look that's truly timeless. Whisper this address to your boyfriend when he needs a tasteful gift-giving idea. He'll love shopping here! And he can't go wrong.

The must-have Hmmm.... Am I really going to divulge my personal lingerie secrets? Well, I won't be giving too much away when I tell you that Fifi's very best undie design is a black lace model she calls "Bel Ami" (you'll find it in the Grands Classiques collection). It's super comfortable, and you can even buy it on the brand's website.

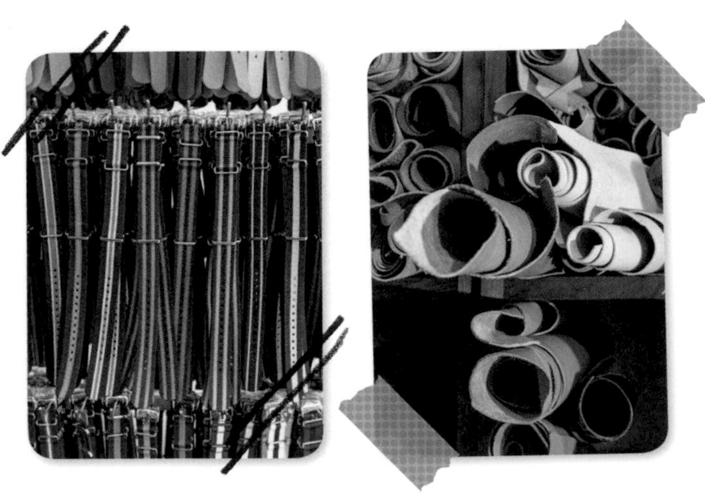

A.B.P. Concept

56, place du Marché-Saint-Honoré, Ier
Tel. +33 (0)1 47 03 49 71 — www.abpparis.com

Why go? Sometimes, the tiniest little thing can make all the difference. Same goes for a watch when you change the band. The Atelier Bracelet Paris boutique specializes in watchbands. A new look also adds value to a budget watch.

The must-have A custom-made band. No one styles you better than you do yourself. This boutique is an *Entreprise du Patrimoine Vivant*, having earned the French distinction of being a "living heritage" business. That's so Parisian!

Say it like La Parisienne

"A good and affordable NATO nylon military wristband (only 20€!) paired with any watch will perform honorably in the service of fashion."

Styl'Honoré

1, rue du Marché-Saint-Honoré, Ier
Tel. +33 (0)1 42 60 43 39

Why go? It's one of Paris's legendary addresses. Here you'll discover treasures that may seem delightfully old-fashioned in this age of smartphones. This is also the place where you'll find one of the last Parisian craftsmen who knows how to cut a quill pen.

→ **The must-have** Inks in an extraordinary array of colors imported from Japan. Or check out the high quality inks produced by Styl'Honoré itself. You'll find all the brands and every price range here.

Say it like La Parisienne

"In an era of e-mails, a handwritten letter is the sign of a rebellious spirit."

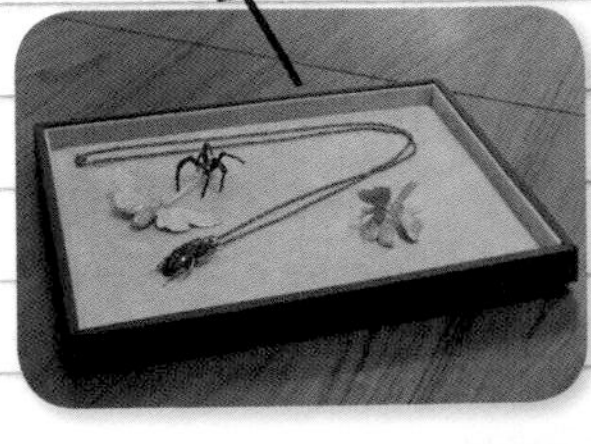

White Bird

38, rue du Mont-Thabor, I[er]
Tel. +33 (0)1 58 62 25 86 — www.whitebirdjewellery.com

Why go? This boutique is home to every hip jewelry designer of the moment, with a penchant for original pieces that break with tradition. That special White Bird find will instantly turn you into a sparkling trendsetter.

→ **The must-have** Chunky rings from the ironically named Pippa Small.

Say it like La Parisienne
"You can never have too much jewelry!"

Astier de Villatte

173, rue Saint-Honoré, Ier
Tel. +33 (0)1 42 60 74 13 — www.astierdevillatte.com

8

Why go? For its vast selection of tableware. There's a design to suit every taste here, including pristine white services for dedicated minimalists. Astier creates ceramics that encompass an array of classic and modern forms.

The must-have If you're not inspired by plates and dishes, pick up a candle or a pretty bottle of eau de cologne. For collectors, there's an incense burner shaped like a cat, designed by the Japanese artist Setsuko Klossowska de Rola exclusively for Astier de Villatte.

Say it like La Parisienne

"Even if you're not much of a cook, you can still dazzle your guests with a gorgeous table setting."

La Corte

320, rue Saint-Honoré, Ier
Tel. +33 (0)1 42 60 45 27 — www.restaurantlacorte.com

Why go? You've had a strenuous morning shopping your way around the neighborhood. A delicious Italian meal is the best way to reinvigorate yourself before resuming the afternoon boutique-crawl.

What to order? Grilled fresh vegetables with a hint of olive oil or maybe taglioni in saffron sauce—everything is great here. For dessert, try the house specialty: a delectable *crème d'amandes avec fraises gratinées* (that's a warm almond-strawberry dessert, to you).

Say it like La Parisienne

"When a restaurant is tucked away in a courtyard, it has to be good to be noticed."

Gourmet Foods/Restaurant

Da Rosa

7, rue Rouget-de-Lisle / 19 bis, rue du Mont-Thabor, Ier
Tel. +33 (0)1 77 37 37 87 — www.darosa.fr

Why go? It's all the rage to enjoy lunch or dinner in a combination *épicerie-cantine* these days. With its red velvet armchairs, this is a very cozy spot indeed. It offers the warm welcome you'd expect from a place that showcases the Mediterranean delights of Italy and Spain. You can count on luxury here as well—Da Rosa is a purveyor to the finest tables of Paris and beyond.

What to order? Bellotta or Parma ham. And don't hesitate to try the Club Sandwich—you can't go wrong at Da Rosa.

Say it like La Parisienne

"I used to go to the left bank Da Rosa (62, rue de Seine, VIe), but I like to cross the river to explore other locations."

Cibus

5, rue Molière, Ier
Tel. +33 (0)1 42 61 50 19

Why go? With just six tables (reservations are de rigueur), this Italian restaurant exclusively features organic food. The place cultivates an aura of mystery that you'll need to get over. It's very cozy and intimate. The food really is delicious, and you'll genuinely swoon over your meal.

What to order? The menu changes constantly. It all depends on what inspires the chef at the fresh food markets. Mozzarella, Parma ham, tiramisu—it's authentic Italian, whatever you choose.

Say it like La Parisienne

"What? You couldn't get a reservation at Cibus? Oh what a shame."

Ines's all-time favorites

12 Delphine Courteille

Hairstylists with real flair

34, rue du Mont-Thabor, Ier
Tel. +33 (0)1 47 03 35 35
www.delphinecourteille.com

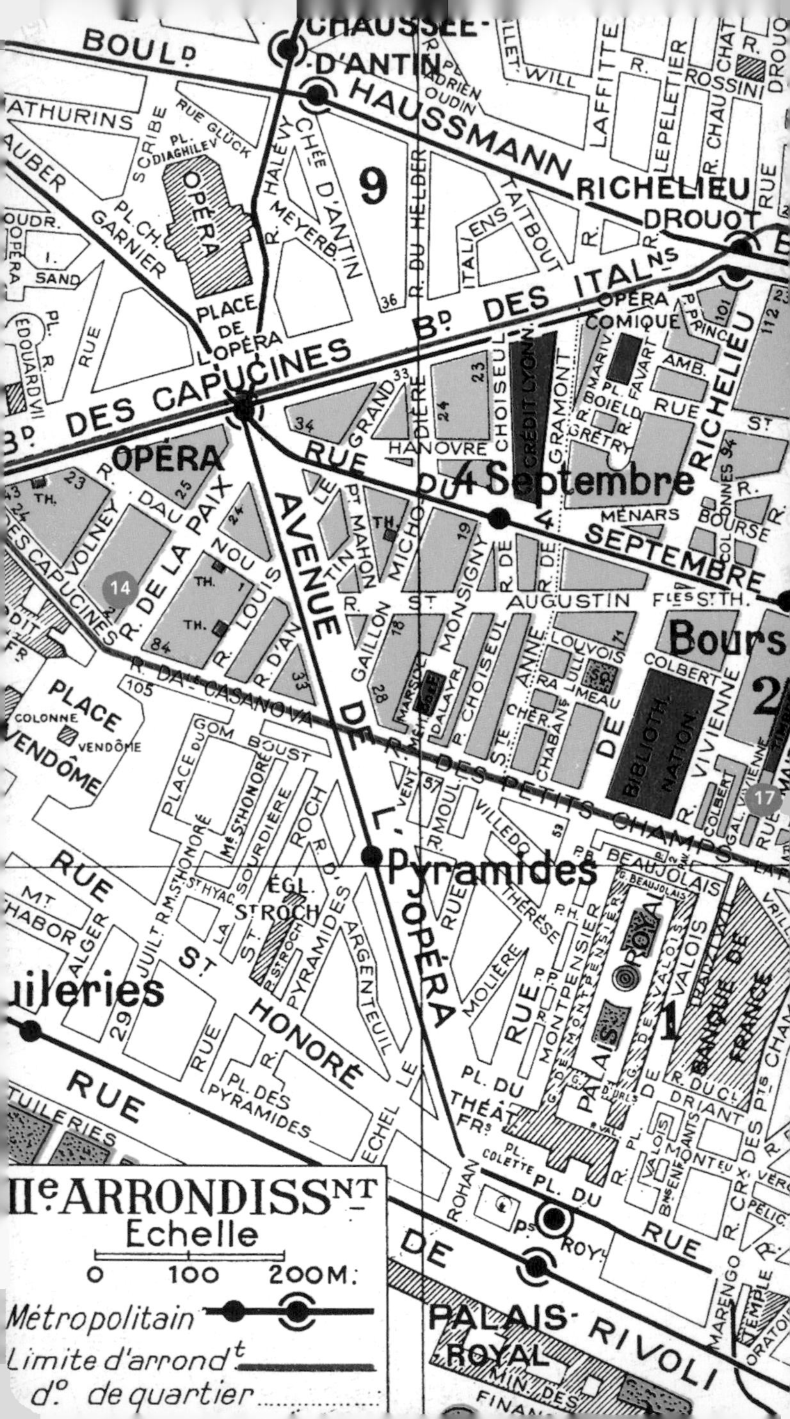

IIe ARRONDISSNT
Echelle
0 100 200M.
Métropolitain
Limite d'arrondt
do de quartier
BOULD HAUSSMANN
CHAUSSÉE-D'ANTIN
RICHELIEU DROUOT
OPÉRA
PLACE DE L'OPÉRA
BD DES CAPUCINES
BD DES ITALNS
OPÉRA COMIQUE
CRÉDIT LYONN.
4 Septembre
RUE DU 4 SEPTEMBRE
AVENUE DE L'OPÉRA
R. DE LA PAIX
PLACE VENDÔME
COLONNE VENDÔME
R. DANL CASANOVA
R. DES PETITS CHAMPS
Bours
BIBLIOTH. NATION.
Pyramides
PALAIS ROYAL
BANQUE DE FRANCE
uileries
RUE ST HONORÉ
EGL. ST ROCH
PL. DES PYRAMIDES
PL. DU THÉAT. FRS
PL. DU PS ROYL
RUE DE RIVOLI
PALAIS-ROYAL
9
2
1

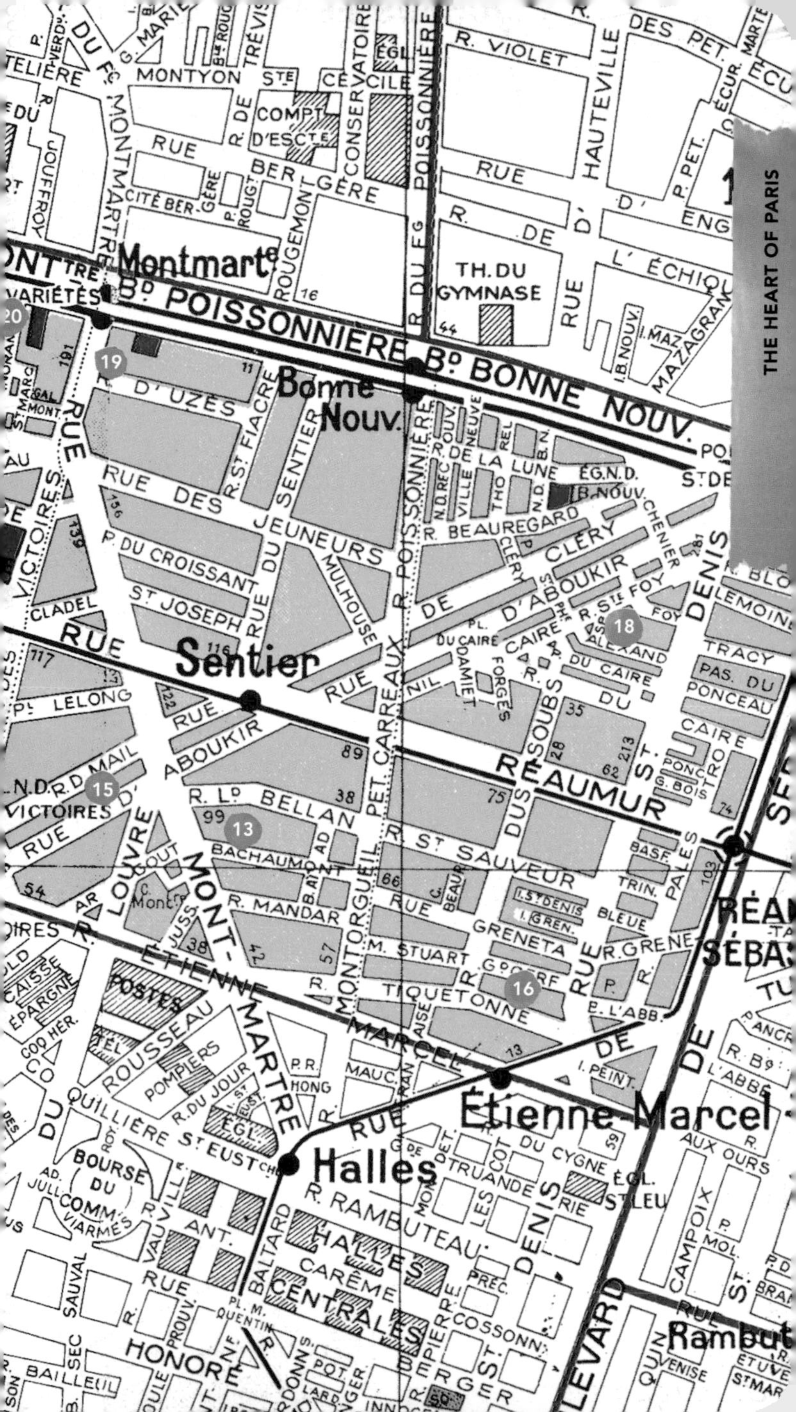

Montmart^e
Bd POISSONNIÈRE
Bd BONNE NOUV.
Bonne Nouv.
Sentier
RÉAUMUR
Étienne-Marcel
Halles
Rambut
RUE BERGÈRE
CONSERVATOIRE
R. DU FG POISSONNIÈRE
RUE D'HAUTEVILLE
R. VIOLET
RUE DES PET. ÉCU
R. DE L'ÉCHIQU
RUE D'ENG
TH. DU GYMNASE
COMPT. D'ESCte
Ste CÉCILE
ÉGL.
MONTYON
CITÉ BERGÈRE
R. ROUGEMONT
P. ROUGT.
RUE MONTMARTRE
VARIÉTÉS
R. D'UZÈS
RUE DES JEUNEURS
RUE DU SENTIER
R. St FIACRE
P. DU CROISSANT
St JOSEPH
RUE DES VICTOIRES
CLADEL
RUE D'ABOUKIR
Pl. LELONG
R. D. MAIL
N.D. VICTOIRES
R. Ld BELLAN
BACHAUMONT
R. MANDAR
RUE MONTORGUEIL
M. STUART
TIQUETONNE
RUE ÉTIENNE MARCEL
MONT-MARTRE
R. DE LA LUNE
ÉG. N.D. B. NOUV.
R. BEAUREGARD
CLÉRY
R. D'ABOUKIR
R. Ste FOY
ALEXAND
DU CAIRE
PL. DU CAIRE
NIL
DAMIET
FORGES
RUE SAINT-DENIS
PAS. DU PONCEAU
CAIRE
TRACY
LEMOINE
MAZAGRAN
R. St SAUVEUR
RUE GRENETA
R. GRENE
BASF.
TRIN.
BLEUE
PALES
R. PET. CARREAUX
R. POISSONNIÈRE
MULHOUSE
POSTES
CAISSE ÉPARGNE
COQ HÉR.
ROUSSEAU
POMPIERS
R. DU JOUR
ÉGL.
QUILLIÈRE St EUST.
BOURSE DU COMM.
VIARMES
RUE SAUVAL
RUE HONORÉ
BAILLEUL
R. RAMBUTEAU
HALLES CENTRALES
CARÊME
COSSONN.
TRUANDERIE
DU CYGNE
ÉGL. St LEU
BOULEVARD DE SÉBASTOPOL
CAMPOIX
AUX OURS
VENISE
P. PEINT.
R. DE L'ABB.
MAUC.
P.R.
HONG
BALTARD
PL. M. QUENTIN
RUE DES LOMBARDS
13
15
16
18
19
20

Salon Christophe Robin

16, rue Bachaumont, IIe

Tel. +33 (0)1 40 20 02 83 — www.christophe-robin.com

Why go? Because Christophe is absolutely the best haircolorist in the world. I'm not the only one to entrust her mane to him: Gisele Bündchen is a client, too.

→ **The must-have** There are several, because Monsieur Robin offers his own range of products. The latest, which promises lightness and shine, is a regenerating hair finish lotion with hibiscus vinegar.

Say it like La Parisienne

"I always book an early morning appointment. That way, I'm not bothered by stars who don't like to get up at dawn."

Amin Kader

1, rue de la Paix, IIᵉ
Tel. +33 (0)1 42 61 33 25 — www.aminkader.fr

Why go? It's worth a trip if only to marvel at the décor of this atmospheric boutique—it will remind you of a Renaissance chapel. Amin Kader has established his identity as a luxury designer while maintaining the freedom to express himself.

The must-have Anything (from bags to pants) from the label will last a lifetime. Among the beauty products on offer, I can't resist the Santa Maria Novella potpourri atomizer.

Say it like La Parisienne

"Amir was the first to offer products from the Officina Santa Maria Novella in Florence, and that's enough to earn my loyalty."

Not Shy: Cashmere Market Outlet

18, rue du Mail, IIe
Tel. +33 (0)1 42 36 99 70 — www.notshy.fr

Why go? Looking for cashmere at rock bottom prices? You simply have to visit this outlet, which, in addition to Uniqlo, also sells stylish, inexpensive cashmere. Not Shy is the new destination where I boldly go ;-). The brand has made its mark with seven hundred outlets in France and abroad.

→ **The must-have** The slogan "The hottest cashmere" gives you a taste of the brand's humor. Its styles may be basic, but Not Shy offers a number of trendy looks every season.

Say it like La Parisienne
"I don't like to overspend on cashmere."

Rickshaw

7, passage du Grand-Cerf, IIe
Tel. +33 (0)1 42 21 41 03 — www.rickshaw.fr

Why go? This shop is an Ali Baba's cave full of treasures imported directly from India. Furniture, decorative accessories of every kind, boxes, and even doorknobs—Indian style melds beautifully with any décor.

The must-have Letters crafted from metal to make a statement on your wall. Indian advertisements on enamel plaques instantly provide a playful, exotic touch to your interior.

Say it like La Parisienne

"Sometimes I don't have time to shop when I'm in Pondicherry. So, when I get back to Paris, I go to Rickshaw."

A NOTRE DAME DES VICTOIRES
·1· EPICERIE P. LEGRAND CONFISERIE ·1·
LEGRAND Filles & Fils

Legrand Filles et Fils

1, rue de la Banque, IIe
Tel. +33 (0)1 42 60 07 12 — www.caves-legrand.com

Why go? It's certainly nothing new—this *épicerie*–wine shop–tasting bar has been around since 1880. But that's the point. You have to admire a place that's been open so long and is still thriving after all these years.

The must-do Why not enroll in one of the courses offered by their wine school, the École du Vin? In just three sessions, you'll be introduced to the essentials of wine tasting. You'll pass for a pro at your next dinner party!

Say it like La Parisienne

"True, they give great advice on wine, but what I like best about Legrand is their redcurrant jam—the seeds are removed by hand using a goose feather."

Edgar

31, rue d'Alexandrie, IIe
Tel. +33 (0)1 40 41 05 19 (hotel)
Tel. +33 (0)1 40 41 05 69 (restaurant) — www.edgarparis.com

Why go? To get away from those impersonal luxury hotels that insist on a dress code. When you're traveling for relaxation and pleasure, you should select your hotel accordingly. Edgar, with its vintage décor, offers a super-cordial welcome in an ideal Paris location.

The room to reserve Everyone knows that Parisian hotel rooms are minuscule. Edgar offers several sizes. Grab the biggest one right away (a deluxe double room at 215 sq. ft. [20 m^2]).

Say it like La Parisienne

"I don't know how many stars this hotel has, but dinner on its restaurant terrace puts stars in my eyes."

Circonstances

174, rue Montmartre, IIe
Tel. +33 (0)1 42 36 17 05 — www.circonstances.fr

Why go? To prove to your significant other that you're *au courant* with restaurants featuring young up-and-coming chefs, not just trendy spots where the entrée comes straight out of the microwave and the music is deafening. Franck (in the kitchen) and Karine (in the dining room)—formerly with the legendary chef Guy Savoy—know exactly what you want: an attractive décor and meals that are distinctive and reliably delicious. This is the sort of place where you could bring a first date, or meet your fiancé's parents. Another point in its favor: the prices are extremely reasonable for a dining experience of this quality.

→ **What to order?** The beef tartare. And the crumble.

Say it like La Parisienne

"I always like restaurants with an open kitchen. If my date turns out to be a dud, at least I can try to master some recipes."

Ines's all-time favorites

20 Racines

The very best of the contemporary bistronomiques

8, passage des Panoramas, IIᵉ
Tel. +33 (0)1 40 13 06 41
www.racinesparis.com

IIIe & IVe
ARRONDISSEMENTS

That Marais State of Mind

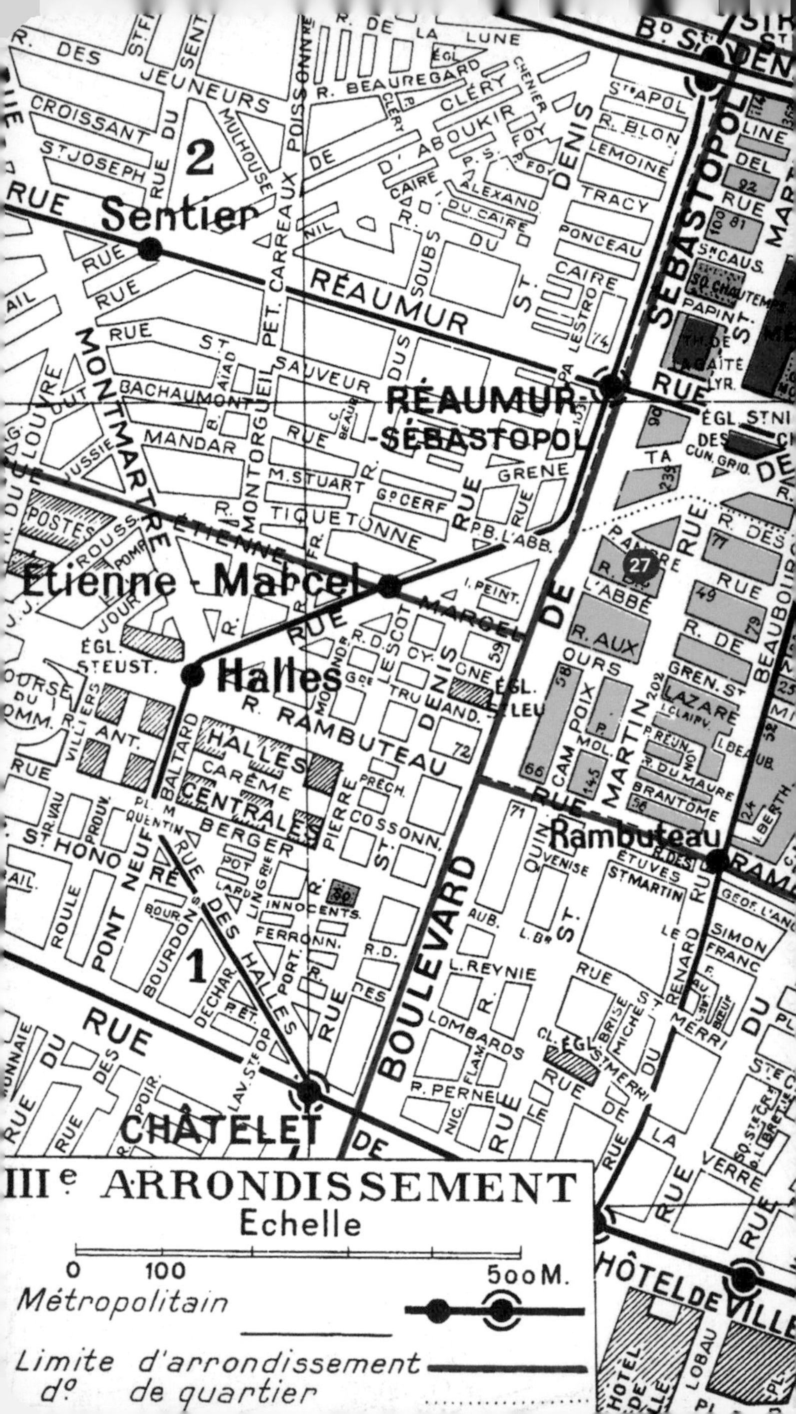

IIIe ARRONDISSEMENT
Echelle
0
100
500 M.
Métropolitain
Limite d'arrondissement
d° de quartier
2
1
Sentier
RÉAUMUR-SÉBASTOPOL
Étienne-Marcel
Halles
Rambuteau
CHÂTELET
HÔTEL DE VILLE
R. DES JEUNEURS
CROISSANT
ST JOSEPH
RUE DU SENTIER
R. DE LA LUNE
R. BEAUREGARD
CLÉRY
D'ABOUKIR
CAIRE
ALEXAND.
DU CAIRE
RUE SAINT DENIS
ST APOL.
R. BLON
LEMOINE
TRACY
PONCEAU
CAIRE
RUE RÉAUMUR
BD ST DENIS
SÉBASTOPOL
RUE MONTMARTRE
RUE ST SAUVEUR
BACHAUMONT
MANDAR
MONTORGUEIL
PET. CARREAUX
POISSONNIÈRE
M. STUART
GD CERF
TIQUETONNE
GRENE
R. ÉTIENNE MARCEL
POSTES
JOUR
ÉGL. ST EUST.
R. RAMBUTEAU
HALLES CENTRALES
BALTARD
CARÊME
BERGER
COSSONN.
INNOCENTS
FERRONN.
LINGERIE
RUE ST HONORÉ
PONT NEUF
ROULE
BOURDONNAIS
RUE DES HALLES
RUE ST DENIS
BOULEVARD DE SÉBASTOPOL
LESCOT
CYGNE
ÉGL. ST LEU
TRUAND.
PRÊCH.
L'ABBÉ
R. AUX OURS
CAM. POIX
RUE ST MARTIN
GREN. ST LAZARE
BRANTOME
RUE QUINCAMPOIX
VENISE
ÉTUVES ST MARTIN
L. REYNIE
LOMBARDS
R. PERNELLE
ÉGL. ST MERRI
RUE DE LA VERRERIE
RENARD
SIMON FRANC
GEOF. L'ANG.
RUE DE RIVOLI
RUE DU BEAUBOURG

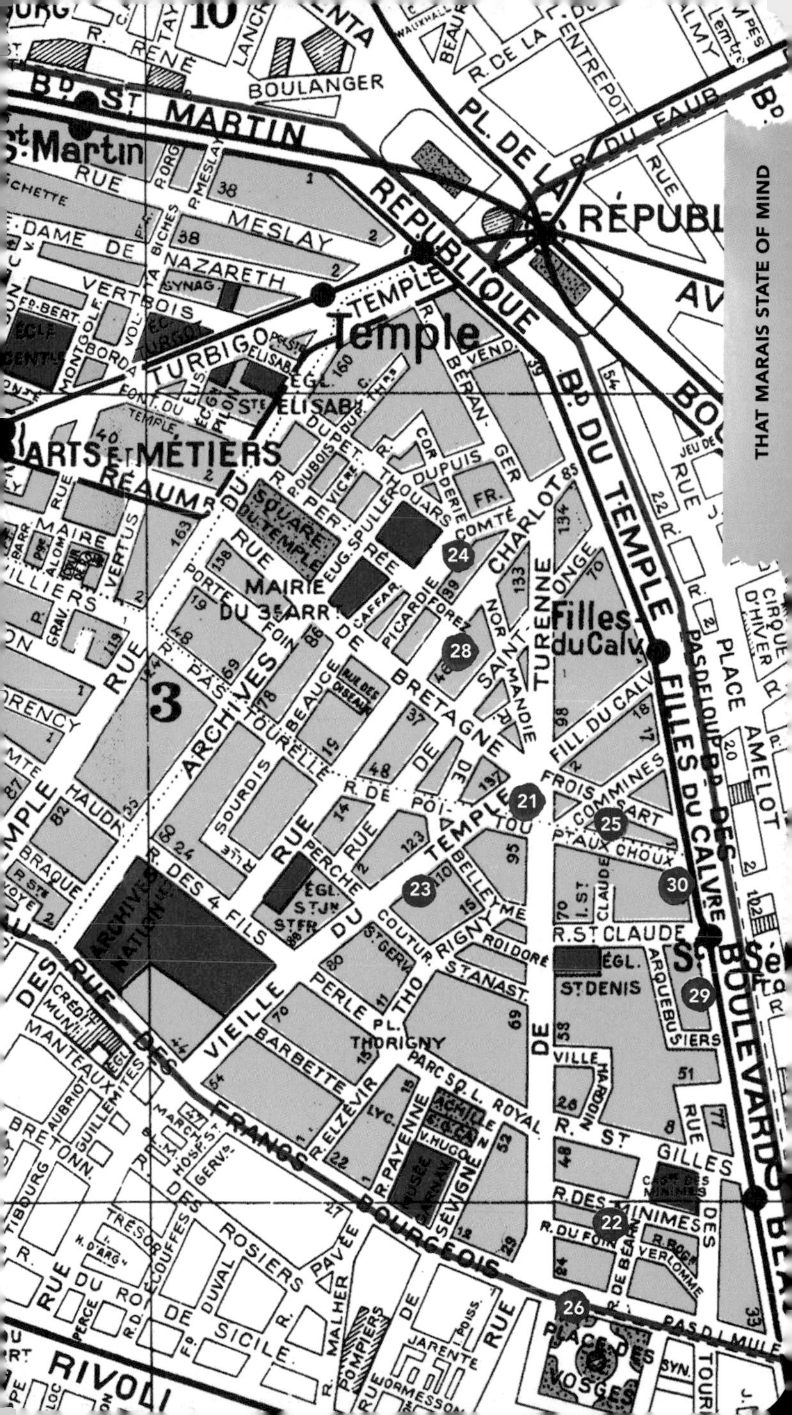

Bd. ST MARTIN
St Martin
PL. DE LA RÉPUBLIQUE
RÉPUBLIQUE
RÉPUBL
R. DU FAUB
R. DE LA
ENTREPOT
BOULANGER
MESLAY
NAZARETH
VERTBOIS
TURBIGO
Temple
TEMPLE
ARTS ET MÉTIERS
RÉAUMUR
SQUARE DU TEMPLE
MAIRIE DU 3E ARR.
Bd DU TEMPLE
Filles du Calv.
FILLES DU CALVAIRE
BOULEVARD
CHARLOT
TURENNE
BRETAGNE
ARCHIVES
RUE DE BRETAGNE
RUE DU TEMPLE
R. DES 4 FILS
VIEILLE DU TEMPLE
ARCHIVES NATIONALES
RUE DES FRANCS BOURGEOIS
BARBETTE
PL. THORIGNY
PARC SQ. L. ROYAL
MUSÉE CARNAVALET
SÉVIGNÉ
R. ST CLAUDE
ÉGL. ST DENIS
RUE ST GILLES
R. DES MINIMES
PLACE DES VOSGES
RUE DES ROSIERS
RUE DU ROI DE SICILE
RIVOLI
PAVÉE
MALHER
AMELOT
24
28
21
25
30
23
29
22
26
3
10

Frenchtrotters

128, rue Vieille-du-Temple, IIIe
Tel. +33 (0)1 44 61 00 14 — www.frenchtrotters.fr

Why go? Carole and Clarent were the first designers to import a number of brands that have gone on to become fashion stars, including Acne. After establishing their concept store, the pair developed their own line. Ultra-trendy, of course.

→ **The must-have** Their men's and women's clothing lines always include t-shirts with quietly elegant messages. The last one that caught our eye: "Simplicity is the ultimate sophistication." It was for men, but that didn't stop us from wearing it.

Say it like La Parisienne
"Frenchtrotters are incredible globetrotters."

Bernard Sylvain

7, rue de Béarn, IIIe
Tel. +33 (0)1 42 78 66 92

Why go? To experience a wonderland. The captivating background music helps to make this boutique a magical world unto itself. Bernard sells jewelry, but he specializes in custom pieces that will make all your jewelry dreams come true. He created a marvelous piece based on one of my ideas.
The must-have A vintage watch, not necessarily from a famous brand, but with a distinctive design.

Say it like La Parisienne
"The most precious gem in this boutique? The owner. He's absolutely charming."

Hod

104, rue Vieille-du-Temple, III[e]
Tel. +33 (0)9 53 15 83 34 — www.hod-boutique.com

Why go? It saves you the trouble of visiting a lot of different shops in search of really special jewelry. This boutique carries all the most sought-after names, from Brooke Gregson to Maria Tash. Some pieces have amazing stories behind them. This shop is the place to find your own good luck charms.

The must-have Taylor Wave's multi-stone Ava ring or anything designed by Dorette.

Say it like La Parisienne

"My necklace is by Sharing. That's the name of a group of Tibetan nuns who've been exiled to Belgium for peacefully demonstrating against the Chinese occupation. You see? Sometimes fashion has its serious side."

Monsieur

53, rue Charlot, IIIe
Tel. +33 (0)1 42 71 12 65 — www.monsieur-paris.com

Why go? It's not easy to find a jewelry atelier like this one. You invariably leave with a little something you just couldn't resist. It's minimalist. And of course it's chic. Monsieur knows how to do simplicity. And designer Nadia Azoug deserves the credit.

The must-have The Zoé ring, a small miracle of delicacy, offered in pink, white, or yellow gold. And the Queen ring, an incomparable design, beautiful in its simplicity.

Say it like La Parisienne

"I was shopping here back in 2009, before you even knew it existed."

MOna MArket

4, rue Commines, IIIe
Tel. +33 (0)1 42 78 80 04 — www.monamarket.com

Why go? To decorate your home. Vases, sheets, lamps, pillows, tableware, children's furnishings—you'll find everything you're looking for. Even some carefully selected clothing, tinted with vegetable dyes.

→ **The must-have** Tinja furniture from Tunisia and the No. 74 clothing line.

Say it like La Parisienne

"I first came across their boutique in Montpellier. It was originally founded by an interior designer who handed over the reins of the Paris shop to her daughter, an interior architect. It's a real family affair."

Tensira

21, place des Vosges, IIIe
Tel. +33 (0)9 83 87 93 10 — www.tensira.com

Why go? You'll need to make an appointment because this is a showroom, not a boutique. I've fallen in love with these fabrics, all handmade in Africa. They're the ultimate in refinement. You'll be head over heels when you see their indigo prints.

The must-have I love the little mattresses. They can be used in so many ways. I sometimes pile them together to create a kind of banquette. You'll also find fabric by the yard, kitchen towels, curtains, and an array of other items crafted from these beautiful textiles.

Say it like La Parisienne

"I never manage to get myself organized to book an appointment with the showroom, so I end up going to all the retailers listed on their website. Great news—even the Ines de la Fressange boutique sells Tensira designs!"

Pep's

Passage de l'Ancre
223, rue Saint-Martin, IIIe
Tel. +33 (0)1 42 78 11 67 — www.peps-paris.com

Why go? This is the kind of atelier-boutique where you feel you have to whisper because it's practically a shrine in this city. You won't find anything at Pep's except umbrellas, parasols, and canes. Most importantly, this is the place to bring your damaged umbrella for repairs. They can even make you a custom-designed brolly!

The must-have Find the perfect umbrella to accessorize your trench coat.

Say it like La Parisienne

"I've got to get in touch with Catherine Deneuve—I'm sure she'd like to repair the Cherbourg umbrella she used on the set of the Jacques Demy movie.

Les Chouettes

32, rue de Picardie, IIIe

Tel. +33 (0)1 44 61 73 21 — www.restaurant-les-chouettes-paris.fr

Why go? To dine in a large, luminous space with floor-to-ceiling windows. The décor is fantastic, from the tile work and seating to the tables and their settings. On sunny days, the outside terrace is packed.

What to order? Everything's very fresh, and the menu changes all the time. Their Paris-Brest pastry is usually available—and it merits a special trip.

Say it like La Parisienne

"Just say 'C'est chouette'*: that's French for 'it's nice'."*

Maison Plisson

93, blvd Beaumarchais, IIIe
Tel. +33 (0)1 71 18 19 09 — www.lamaisonplisson.com

Why go? For the grocery selection. This 5,400-square-foot (500-m^2) space encompasses a market, a wine cellar, a bakery, and a restaurant featuring an outside terrace. It's the new hot spot, opened by a gal with a background in the fashion business. Needless to say, the space is skillfully designed. That's a plus, considering that it's not far from Merci, that fabulous concept store (111, blvd Beaumarchais, IIIe).

What to order? Everything here is good, because Delphine Plisson carefully selects her suppliers, producers, and farmers. And the bonus? They offer home delivery.

Say it like La Parisienne

"It reminds me of New York, because it's actually open on Sunday."

Ines's all-time favorites

30 Merci

The coolest, chicest concept store

111, blvd Beaumarchais, IIIe
Tel. +33 (0)1 42 77 00 33
www.merci-merci.com

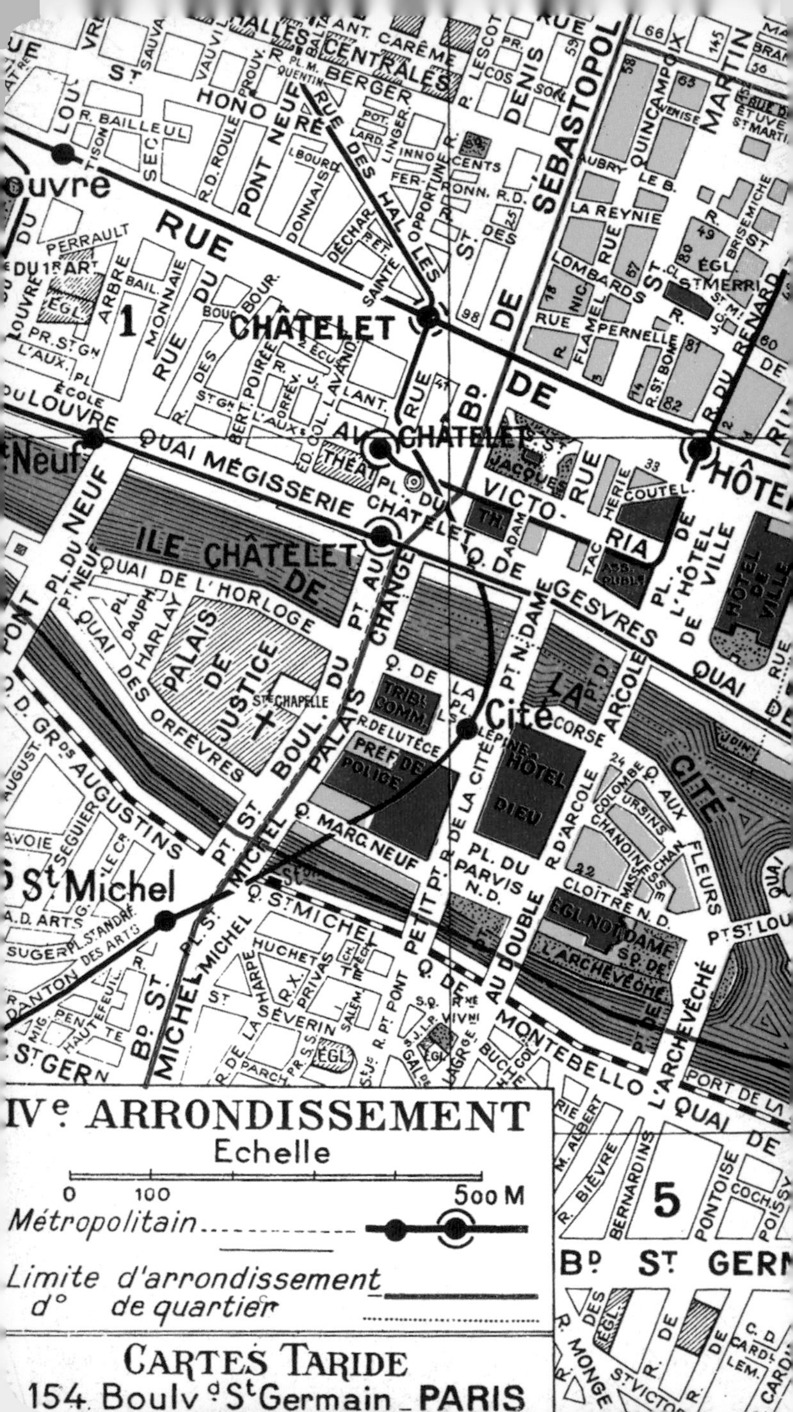

IVe ARRONDISSEMENT
Echelle
0
100
500 M
Métropolitain
Limite d'arrondissement
d° de quartier
CARTES TARIDE
154. Boulvd St Germain _ PARIS
HALLES CENTRALES
RUE DE RIVOLI
CHÂTELET
BD DE SÉBASTOPOL
AV. VICTORIA
HÔTEL DE VILLE
QUAI MÉGISSERIE
ILE DE LA CITÉ
PALAIS DE JUSTICE
STE CHAPELLE
PRÉF. DE POLICE
HÔTEL DIEU
ÉGL. NOTRE DAME
PL. DU PARVIS N.D.
QUAI DE GESVRES
QUAI DES ORFÈVRES
QUAI DES GDS AUGUSTINS
St Michel
BD ST MICHEL
QUAI DE MONTEBELLO
BD ST GERM
PONT NEUF
Louvre

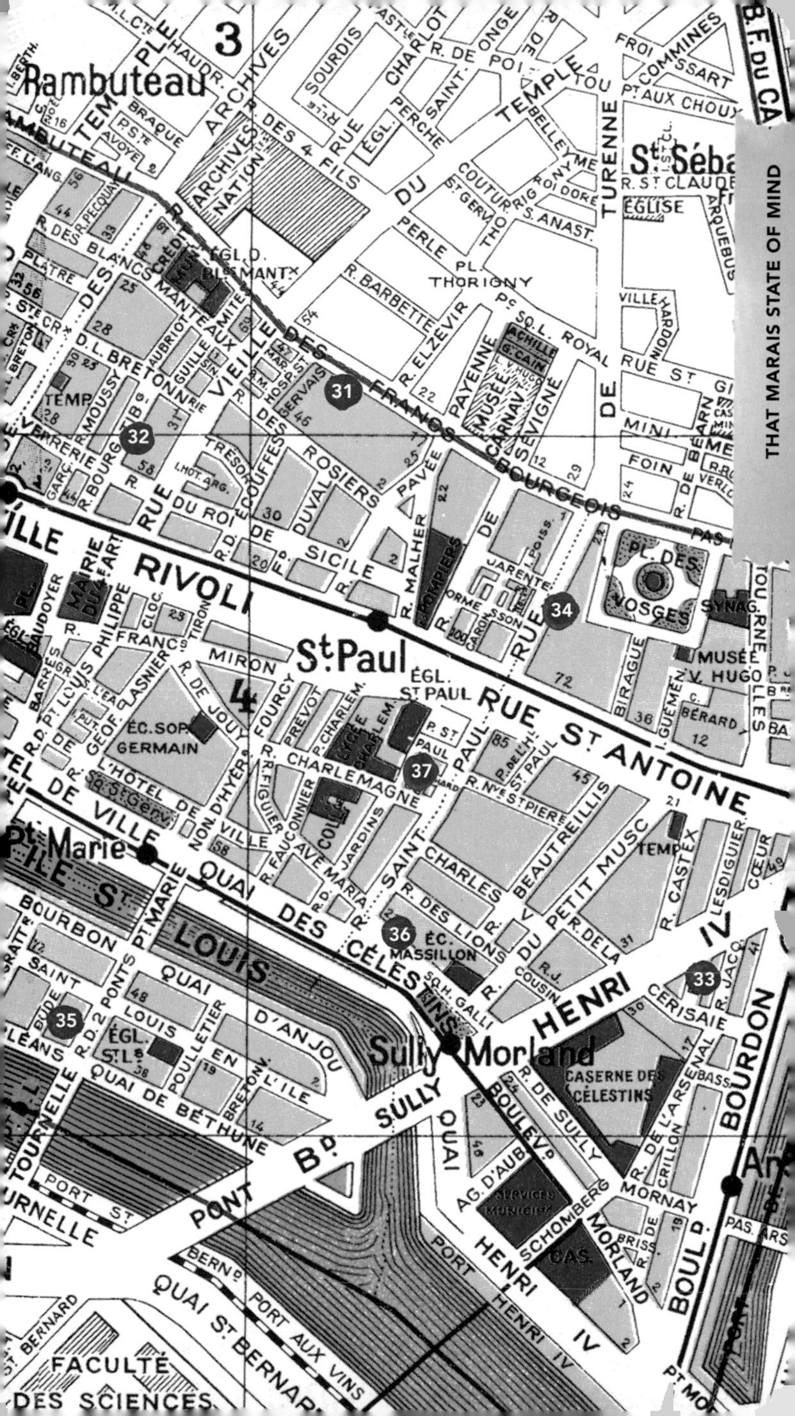
3
4
Rambuteau
St Paul
Pt Marie
Sully Morland
31
32
33
34
35
36
37
R. DES 4 FILS
ARCHIVES NATION.
RUE DU TEMPLE
TURENNE
St Sébas
R. ST CLAUDE
PERLE
PL. THORIGNY
R. BARBETTE
R. ELZÉVIR
PAYENNE
MUSÉE CARNAVALET
SÉVIGNÉ
SQ. L. ROYAL
DES FRANCS BOURGEOIS
R. DES BLANCS MANTEAUX
VIEILLE DU TEMPLE
STE CROIX DE LA BRETONNERIE
TEMP.
VERRERIE
R. BOURG TIBOURG
ROSIERS
R. PAVÉE
R. MALHER
POMPIERS
RUE DU ROI DE SICILE
R. DE JARENTE
PL. DES VOSGES
SYNAG.
MUSÉE V. HUGO
RIVOLI
MAIRIE DU 4E ART
MIRON
ÉGL. ST PAUL
RUE ST ANTOINE
R. FRANÇOIS MIRON
ÉC. SOP. GERMAIN
L'HÔTEL DE VILLE
R. DE JOUY
FOURCY
PREVOT
LYCÉE CHARLEM.
R. CHARLEMAGNE
R. ST PAUL
BIRAGUE
BEAUTREILLIS
R. DU PETIT MUSC
R. CASTEX
TEMP.
R. DES JARDINS ST PAUL
AVE MARIA
R. ST CHARLES
R. DES LIONS
ÉC. MASSILLON
QUAI DES CÉLESTINS
ILE ST LOUIS
QUAI DE BOURBON
QUAI D'ANJOU
R. ST LOUIS EN L'ILE
ÉGL. ST L.
QUAI DE BÉTHUNE
POULLETIER
TOURNELLE
PONT SULLY
BD HENRI IV
CERISAIE
CASERNE DES CÉLESTINS
R. DE SULLY
BOULEVD MORLAND
R. DE L'ARSENAL
MORNAY
SCHOMBERG
SERVICES MUNICIPX
BOURDON
BOULD BOURDON
QUAI HENRI IV
PORT HENRI IV
PORT ST BERNARD
PORT AUX VINS
QUAI ST BERNARD
FACULTÉ DES SCIENCES

Uniqlo

39, rue des Francs-Bourgeois, IVᵉ
Tel. +33 (0)1 53 01 87 87 — www.uniqlo.com

Why go? Because when you're looking for high-quality basics at a very good price, you can't do better than Uniqlo. And I was saying that to everybody even before I started designing collections for them. Check it out for yourself; the Uniqlo boutique in the Marais is terrific.

→ **The must-have** Go ahead and explore. Don't be afraid to shop in the men's section for loose fitting linen shirts and jeans. Their pullovers look great for those days when you want to come across as relaxed and hip.

Say it like La Parisienne

"Top quality at low prices—only origami champions like the Japanese could get that mix right."

La Botte Gardiane

25, rue du Bourg-Tibourg, IVe
Tel. +33 (0)1 77 16 58 45 — www.labottegardiane.com

Why go? There was widespread jubilation when these boots became available in Paris. Until the two shops opened here, you had to take the train to the south of France to wrangle a pair of *bottes gardianes*. This traditional footwear is de rigueur for the cowboys who herd bulls and wild horses in the Camargue. But don't worry, you can still wear the boots, even without a horse.

The must-have The original *bottes gardianes*. But the new Belle-Île sandals are also worth a try.

Say it like La Parisienne

"I ordered custom-designed Camarguais boots They're beige-colored, fur-lined, and quite tall. I hope I don't have to wait too long for them—they're perfect for winter shopping expeditions."

Bird on the Wire

2, rue de Lesdiguières, IVe
Tel. +33 (0)1 42 74 83 79 — www.botw.fr

Why go? When you need gift-giving inspiration—especially for grown-ups. The shop is brimming with whimsical gadgets, playful costume jewelry, paper napkins, and even soup ladles.

→ **The must-have** A cosmetic case that reminds you that "A smile is the best makeup to wear"… or the Mr. Wonderful coffee mug that promises super powers against raccoon eyes.

Say it like La Parisienne
"You can never have too many coasters."

forever

Delphine Pariente

19, rue de Turenne, IV[e]
Tel. +33 (0)1 42 71 84 64 — www.delphinepariente.fr

Why go? You'll find adorable jewelry at bargain prices because a lot of the items are gold plated. When one of my friends has a baby, I give her a little pendant necklace or a personalized medallion, with a matching one for the bambino. Because she already received twenty-three Bonpoint baby sweaters and thirty-five cuddly stuffed animals.

→ **The must-have** The Bambi pendant. I love deer—they're my animal fetish. My house is full of them, and so is my boutique.

Say it like La Parisienne

"Instead of bringing flowers as a hostess gift, I come bearing rings. They last longer!"

"YOU'LL EVEN SEE HOME-SICK JAPANESE VISITORS AT ISAMI. THAT GIVES YOU AN IDEA OF THE RESTAURANT'S AUTHEN-TICITY."

Isami

4, quai d'Orléans, IVᵉ
Tel. +33 (0)1 40 46 06 97

Why go? It's not the best-known Japanese restaurant in Paris, but it's certainly got the best location, right on the Île Saint-Louis. And some claim it has the finest sushi in Paris. You'll need to reserve a seat at the bar to see the chef at work.

What to order? I can't remember the names of the dishes—they're too complicated. Whatever you order, make sure you get the raw fish—you'll rarely find more delicious sushi anywhere.

Le Petit Célestin

12, quai des Célestins, IVe
Tel. +33 (0)1 73 20 25 24 — www.lepetitcelestin.fr

Why go? For that "Only in Paris" experience. Overlooking the Seine, this restaurant comes across as a thoroughly authentic bistro. It's a delightful place, and we love those traditional red-and-white checked napkins. In the summertime, inviting outside tables add to the charm.

→ **What to order?** Everything here is simple and good, from the cherry tomatoes with burrata to the tuna tartare.

Say it like La Parisienne
"Now that's the real Paris!"

Ines's all-time favorites

37 Cru

The restaurant with the best outdoor terrace in Paris

7, rue Charlemagne, IVe
Tel. +33 (0)1 40 27 81 84
www.restaurantcru.fr

Ve ARRONDISSEMENT

The Latin Quarter

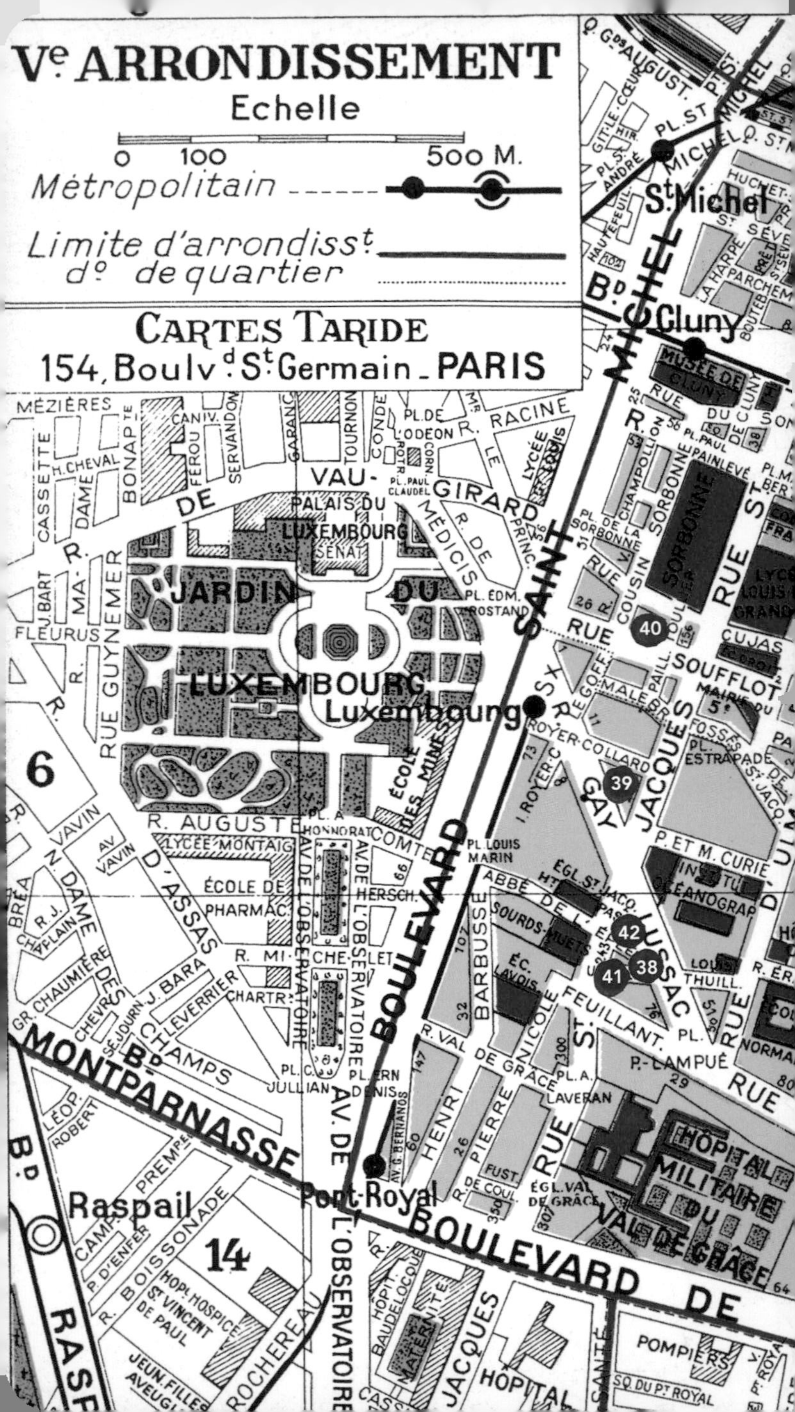
Ve ARRONDISSEMENT
Echelle
0 100 500 M.
Métropolitain
Limite d'arrondisst
do de quartier
CARTES TARIDE
154, Boulvd St Germain _ PARIS
Bd St MICHEL
St Michel
Cluny
MUSÉE DE CLUNY
RUE DU SOMMERARD
R. RACINE
PL. DE L'ODEON
LYCÉE St LOUIS
SORBONNE
PL. DE LA SORBONNE
R. CHAMPOLLION
RUE CUJAS
RUE SOUFFLOT
MAIRIE DU 5e
PL. PAUL PAINLEVÉ
R. DE VAUGIRARD
PALAIS DU LUXEMBOURG
SÉNAT
JARDIN DU LUXEMBOURG
Luxembourg
R. DE MÉDICIS
PL. EDM. ROSTAND
RUE GAY LUSSAC
RUE ST JACQUES
R. ROYER-COLLARD
PL. ESTRAPADE
P. ET M. CURIE
INSTITUT OCÉANOGRAP.
R. AUGUSTE COMTE
LYCÉE MONTAIGNE
ÉCOLE DE PHARMAC.
ÉCOLE DES MINES
BOULEVARD SAINT MICHEL
AV. DE L'OBSERVATOIRE
R. MICHELET
PL. LOUIS MARIN
ABBÉ DE L'ÉPÉE
EGL. ST JACQ. HT PAS
SOURDS-MUETS
RUE HENRI BARBUSSE
R. VAL DE GRÂCE
FEUILLANT.
PL. A. LAVERAN
RUE PIERRE NICOLE
HÔPITAL MILITAIRE DU VAL DE GRÂCE
ÉGL. VAL DE GRÂCE
BOULEVARD DE PORT-ROYAL
Port-Royal
Bd MONTPARNASSE
Raspail
Bd RASPAIL
R. BOISSONADE
HOPL. HOSPICE ST VINCENT DE PAUL
JEUN. FILLES AVEUGLES
MATERNITÉ
HÔPITAL
POMPIERS
SQ. DU Pt ROYAL
R. D'ASSAS
R. GUYNEMER
R. DE FLEURUS
R. VAVIN
R. N. DAME DES CHAMPS
6
14
40
39
42
41
38

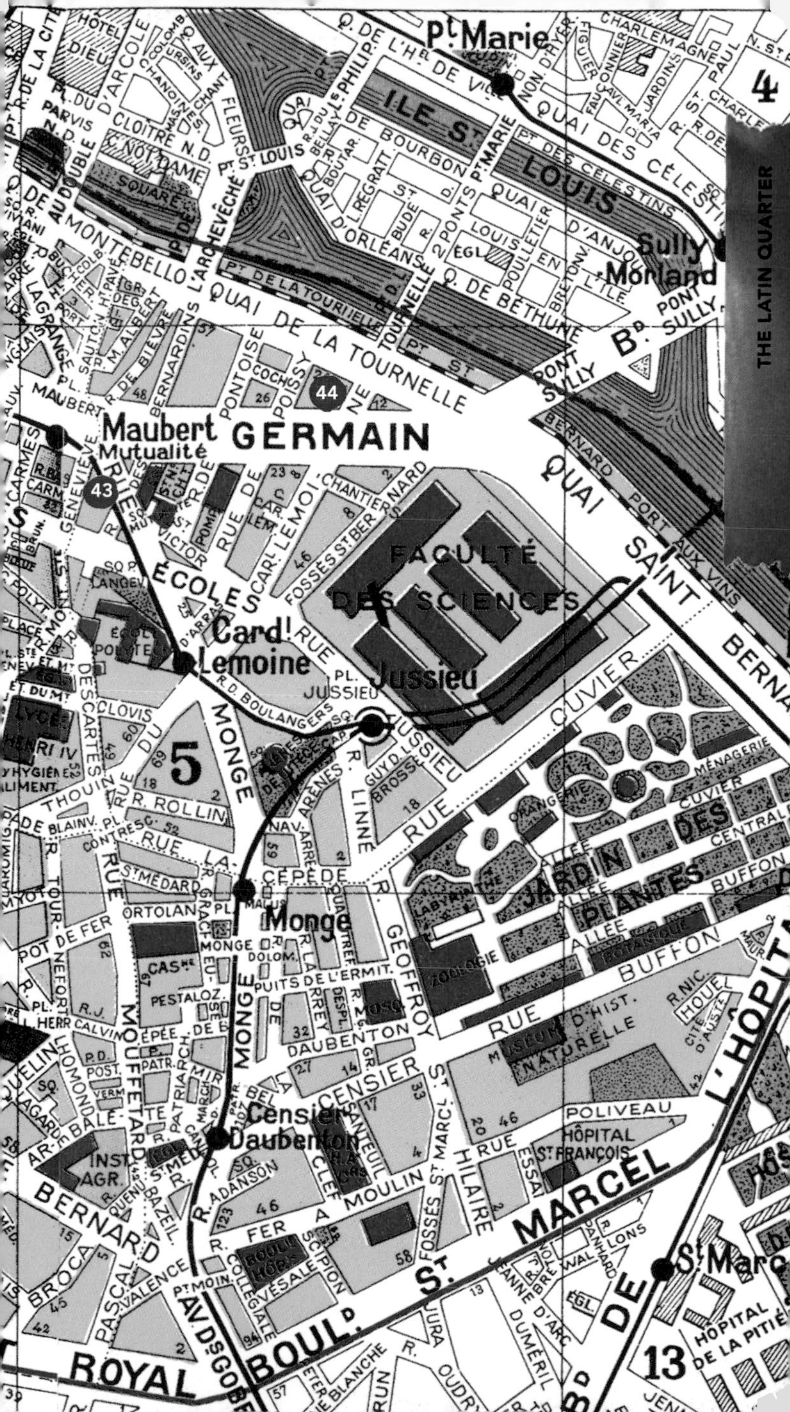
THE LATIN QUARTER
4
5
13
Pt. Marie
ILE St. LOUIS
QUAI DES CÉLESTINS
Sully Morland
PONT SULLY
Bd. SULLY
QUAI D'ANJOU
QUAI D'ORLÉANS
Q. DE BÉTHUNE
QUAI DE BOURBON
Pt. DE LA TOURNELLE
QUAI DE LA TOURNELLE
QUAI DE MONTEBELLO
Pt. St. LOUIS
HOTEL DIEU
PARVIS N.D.
SQUARE
Maubert Mutualité
GERMAIN
43
44
QUAI SAINT BERNARD
PORT AUX VINS
FACULTÉ DES SCIENCES
Jussieu
Card l. Lemoine
ÉCOLES
ÉCOLE POLYTECH.
LYCÉE HENRI IV
MONGE
Monge
RUE CUVIER
JARDIN DES PLANTES
MÉNAGERIE
ORANGERIE
LABYRINTHE
ZOOLOGIE
BOTANIQUE
ALLÉE BUFFON
RUE BUFFON
MUSÉUM D'HIST. NATURELLE
RUE GEOFFROY
R. LINNÉ
RUE THOUIN
R. ROLLIN
RUE LACÉPÈDE
RUE MOUFFETARD
POT DE FER
ORTOLAN
PESTALOZ.
DAUBENTON
CENSIER
Censier Daubenton
POLIVEAU
HÔPITAL St FRANÇOIS
Bd. St. MARCEL
St Marcel
HÔPITAL DE LA PITIÉ
BOUL. DE L'HÔPITAL
INST. AGR.
BERNARD
BROCA
PASCAL
VALENCE
AV. DES GOBELINS
ROYAL
BOUL.
FER A MOULIN
SCIPION
VÉSALE
COLLÉGIALE
R. ADANSON
JEANNE D'ARC
DUMÉRIL
R. DE CLEF
R. St HILAIRE
FOSSÉS St MARCEL

Breiz-Norway

33, rue Gay-Lussac, V^{e}
Tel. +33 (0)1 43 29 47 82

38

Why go? Everybody needs a real cotton boatneck sailor's top. And maybe a sailor's cap or some thick woolen socks. When you're looking for an outfit from Brittany or Norway, this is the place to go.

The must-have The indispensable sailor top to wear year-round. It survives passing time and trends, and never changes its stripes!

Say it like La Parisienne

"My sailor tops? I get them straight from the source."

Finn-Austria

25, rue Gay-Lussac, Ve
Tel. +33 (0)1 43 54 75 40 — www.finn-austria.fr

39

Why go? In traditional Austrian attire, it's easy to get that folkloric look. And you don't have to travel to Austria or go to the Viennese opera to stock up. This boutique was established at the initiative of the Austrian embassy to promote the country's products.

The must-have A jacquard pullover, to look like Ingrid Bergman dressed for winter sports.

Say it like La Parisienne

"Doesn't my Austrian hunting jacket remind you of a Chanel?"

Dubois

20, rue Soufflot, Ve
Tel. +33 (0)1 44 41 67 50 — www.dubois-paris.com

Why go? You can never have enough notebooks. I contracted a notebook fixation, and hoard them as if a catastrophic stationery shortage was imminent. This shop specializes in fine art supplies. It was founded in 1861, which means you can count on high quality in this emporium.
The must-have A Kaweco pen—mine is made of copper. And caps for my pencils.

Say it like La Parisienne
"In times of stress, this is where I go for coloring books. You've heard of art therapy, right?"

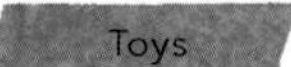

Bass et Bass

8, rue de l'Abbé-de-L'Épée, Ve — Tel. +33 (0)1 42 25 97 01
and **La Boutique Bass: 229, rue Saint-Jacques, Ve**
Tel. +33 (0)1 43 25 52 52 — www.bassetbass.fr

Why go? Toyshops that sell wooden and metal toys are always appealing. Although, I admit that I love colorful plastic toys, too—in fact I sell them in my boutique. Bass et Bass's wooden toys are new, but they have a retro feel. Old-fashioned playthings are all the rage in this era of video games.
→ **The must-have** Metal toys that you wind up with a key—a merry-go-round, robot, or elephant, to mention just a few.

Say it like La Parisienne
"I often give nice wooden toys as gifts; if the child isn't interested in playing with them, they still look great as bedroom decorations."

"A BEAUTIFUL BOUQUET ALLOWS YOU TO FORGET THAT THE HOUSE NEEDS CLEANING."

Thalie

223, rue Saint-Jacques, Ve
Tel. +33 (0)1 43 54 41 00 — www.thalie-fleurs.fr

Why go? Beautiful flower arrangements have a lot in common with gourmet meals. They both require top-quality ingredients put together by an accomplished artist. That's exactly what you'll find at Pascale Leray's Thalie. She carries magnificent anemones, sweetpeas, and flowering plants, along with an incredible variety of other blooms. You can count on her to make gorgeous arrangements for special events (your wedding, for example). They'll create a sensation!

The must-have I especially love pale pink poppies. And violets—I named my daughter Violette. Luckily for her, I don't like tulips!

Aux Merveilleux de Fred

2, rue Monge, V^e^
Tel. +33 (0)1 43 54 63 72 — www.auxmerveilleux.com

Why go? There aren't many pâtisseries where the star attractions are just two cakes: one white (the *Incroyable*, meringue and speculos-flavored whipped cream, covered with white chocolate shavings) and the other black (the *Merveilleux*, meringue and bittersweet chocolate whipped cream, covered with dark chocolate shavings). They're the stars at all our family birthday celebrations. These original confections now have some company, including the cherry-flavored *Excentrique* and the caramel *Sans-Culotte*.

→ **What to order?** People come primarily for the aptly-named "marvelous" and "incredible" cakes.

Say it like La Parisienne

"When I'm in New York and need a sugar high, I head for the Aux Merveilleux shop on Eighth Avenue."

Chez René

14, blvd Saint-Germain, V[e]
Tel. +33 (0)1 43 54 30 23

Why go? It's a well-known fact that everything created in 1957 is top notch. (It also happens to be the year I was born!) This restaurant is no exception. The terrace is lovely during the summer months and it's the perfect spot for anyone who wants to feel at home in the "real" France. The traditional décor features old posters and the menu is classic—and good. It's the ideal venue for foreign visitors who are after an "authentic" French experience.

What to order? *Tournedos de rumsteak, pot au feu, quenelles de brochet*—you get the point. It's 100% classic French.

Say it like La Parisienne

"I know it's a restaurant for real men when I see rognons de veau *on the menu!"*

VIe & VIIe
ARRONDISSEMENTS

Saint-Germain-des-Prés Style

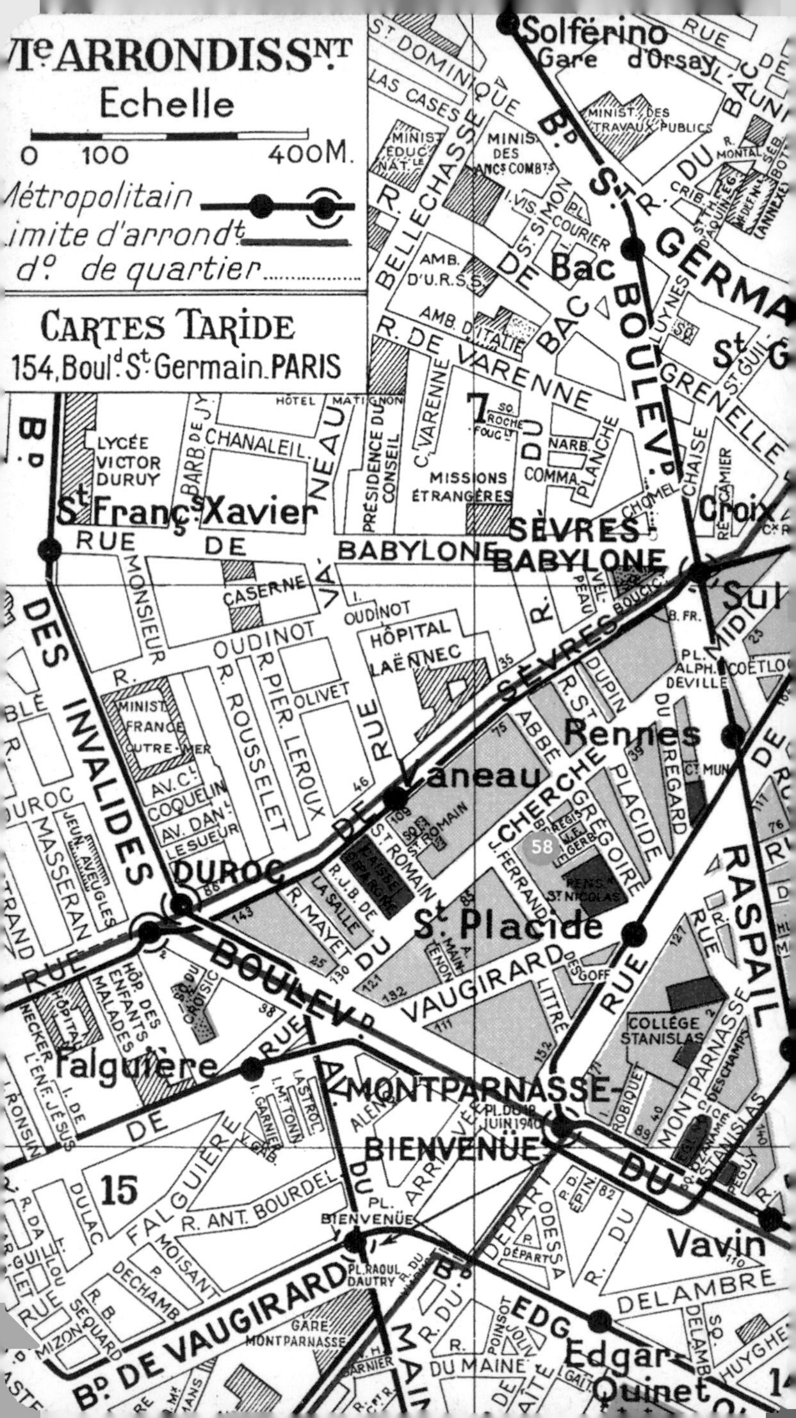

VIIe ARRONDISSt.

Echelle

0 100 400M.

Métropolitain

Limite d'arrondt.

do. de quartier

CARTES TARIDE

154, Bould. St. Germain, PARIS

Solférino
Gare d'Orsay
Bac
Sèvres Babylone
St. Franç.s Xavier
Vaneau
Duroc
St. Placide
Rennes
Falguière
Montparnasse-Bienvenüe
Vavin
Edgar-Quinet
Croix

R. St. Dominique
Las Cases
R. Bellechasse
R. de Bac
Bd. St. Germain
Boulevd. Raspail
R. de Varenne
R. de Grenelle
Rue de Babylone
R. Vaneau
Rue Monsieur
R. Oudinot
Bd. des Invalides
R. Rousselet
R. Pier. Leroux
Rue de Sèvres
Boulevd. du Montparnasse
Rue du Cherche Midi
R. de Vaugirard
Rue de Rennes
Rue du Regard
R. Duroc
Masseran
Bd. de Vaugirard
Rue Falguière
R. Ant. Bourdel
R. du Départ
R. d'Odessa
Delambre
R. du Maine
Littré
R. Mayet
Bd. Edg. Quinet

Minist. Educ. Nat.le
Minist. des Ancs Combts
Minist. des Travaux Publics
Amb. d'U.R.S.S.
Amb. d'Italie
Hôtel Matignon
Présidence du Conseil
Missions Étrangères
Lycée Victor Duruy
Caserne
Hôpital Laënnec
Minist. France Outre-Mer
Hôp. des Enfants Malades
Hôpital Necker
Collège Stanislas
Gare Montparnasse
Pl. du 18 Juin 1940
Pl. Bienvenüe
Pl. Raoul Dautry
Pl. Alph. Deville
Jeun. Aveugles

7

15

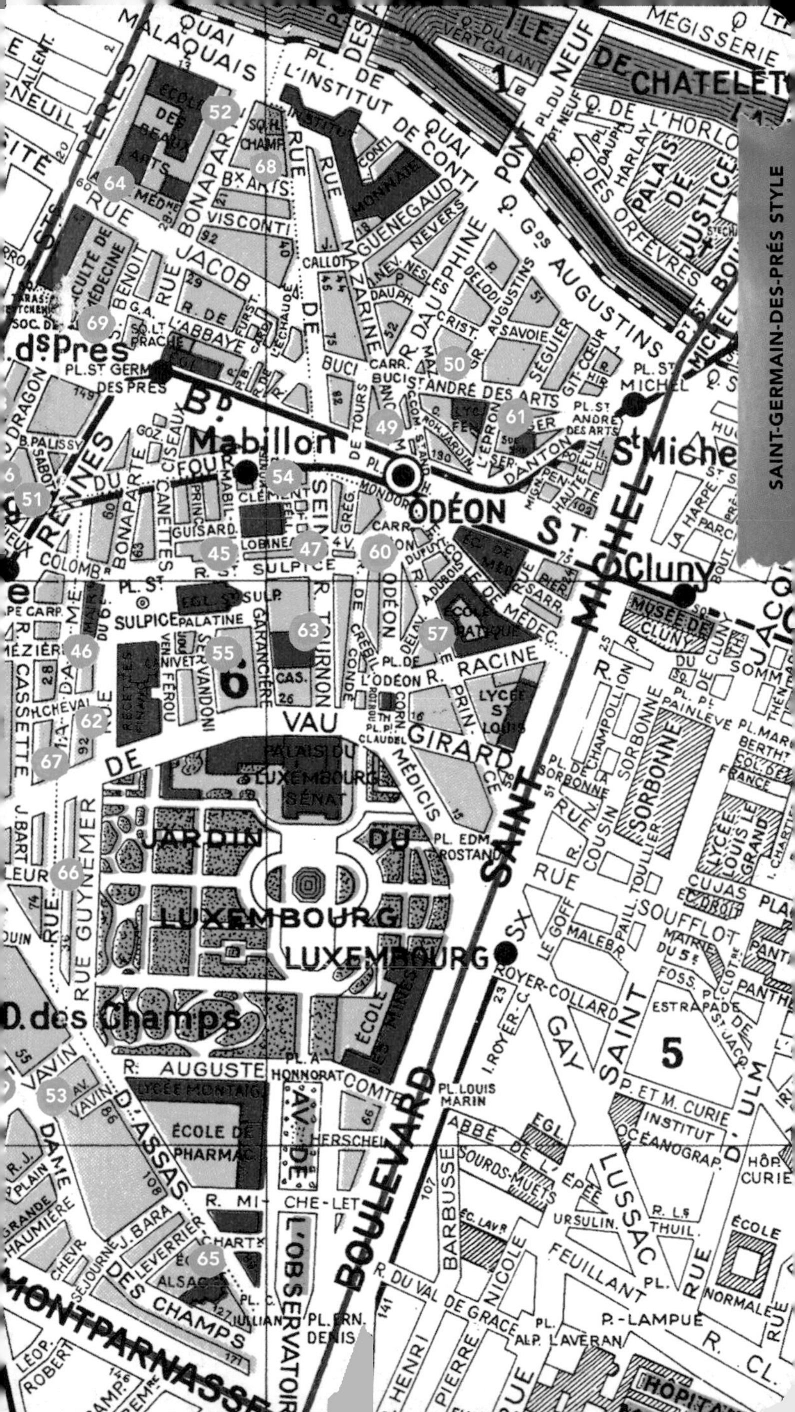
QUAI MALAQUAIS
PL. DE L'INSTITUT
QUAI DE CONTI
Q. DU VERT GALANT
ÎLE DE
CHATELET
MÉGISSERIE
PONT NEUF
Q. DE L'HORLOGE
Q. DES ORFÈVRES
PALAIS DE JUSTICE
Q. GDS AUGUSTINS
ÉCOLE DES BEAUX ARTS
INSTITUT
MONNAIE
RUE BONAPARTE
RUE JACOB
VISCONTI
BX ARTS
RUE MAZARINE
RUE DE SEINE
GUÉNÉGAUD
NEVERS
R. DAUPHINE
FACULTÉ DE MÉDECINE
R. DE L'ABBAYE
PL. ST GERMAIN DES PRES
BUCI
SAVOIE
SÉGUIER
ST ANDRÉ DES ARTS
PL. ST MICHEL
Bd Mabillon
FOUR
ODÉON
St Michel
DANTON
RENNES
CANETTES
CISEAUX
GUISARD.
LOBINEAU
R. ST SULPICE
PL. ST SULPICE
EGL. ST SULP.
PALATINE
SERVANDONI
GARANCIÈRE
R. TOURNON
ODÉON
R. DE CONDÉ
ÉCOLE DE MÉDEC.
St
Cluny
MUSÉE DE CLUNY
R. RACINE
LYCÉE ST LOUIS
PL. DE L'ODÉON
VAU
GIRARD
MÉDICIS
PALAIS DU LUXEMBOURG SÉNAT
JARDIN DU
LUXEMBOURG
LUXEMBOURG
SAINT
MICHEL
SORBONNE
PL. DE LA SORBONNE
CHAMPOLLION
R. CUJAS
SOUFFLOT
LYCÉE LOUIS LE GRAND
COL. DE FRANCE
RUE GUYNEMER
R. CASSETTE
RUE MADAME
D.des Champs
VAVIN
R. AUGUSTE COMTE
AV. DE L'OBSERVATOIRE
ÉCOLE DE PHARMAC.
R. MICHELET
D'ASSAS
ÉCOLE DES MINES
BOULEVARD
ROYER-COLLARD
GAY LUSSAC
RUE SAINT JACQUES
5
P. ET M. CURIE
INSTITUT OCÉANOGRAP.
RUE D'ULM
ABBÉ DE L'ÉPÉE
SOURDS-MUETS
FEUILLANT
RUE NICOLE
BARBUSSE
R. DU VAL DE GRACE
PL. ALP. LAVERAN
PIERRE
HENRI
MONTPARNASSE
DES CHAMPS
LEVERRIER
ÉCOLE NORMALE
HÔPITAL
52
68
64
69
50
61
49
54
51
45
47
60
46
55
63
57
62
67
66
53
65
6

Tabio

32, rue Saint-Sulpice, VIe
Tel. +33 (0)1 43 26 28 12 — www.tabio.fr

Why go? If your family members go to battle over a pair of socks when ownership has become a bit hazy, just head over to Tabio, where they embroider monograms onto fancy footwear—guaranteed to reestablish household harmony. Only the Japanese could dream up such a brilliant idea.

The must-have You have to be daring and select original patterns. But skip the five-toe rainbow model.

Say it like La Parisienne

"I never buy anything but fuchsia-colored socks. That way, no one ever steals them."

Milk on the Rocks

7, rue de Mézières, VIe
Tel. +33 (0)1 45 49 19 84 — www.milkontherocks.net

Why go? Imaginative details, rock'n'roll prints, surprising colors, and comfortable fabrics—Milk on the Rocks makes clothing that pleases children just as much as parents. It's great because you can bring the kids along on this shopping expedition. The boutique is full of gadgets to amuse youngsters.

→ **The must-have** T-shirts emblazoned with a lion or panda head (depending on the collection) and sweatshirts that always have fun motifs.

Say it like La Parisienne

"I'm eternally grateful to Milk on the Rocks for designing an anise-green cardigan with turquoise trim in a children's size 16. I can fit into it, and I love its vintage look."

Wild

18, rue Saint-Sulpice, VIe
Tel. +33 (0)1 43 54 76 22 — www.wild-paris.com

Why go? Everything here is in shades of beige, off-white, and taupe. The look is boho chic. Right away you'll want to unleash your inner Pocahontas and don some fringed moccasins or a pair of well-worn cowboy boots.

→ **The must-have** A desert-style scarf that looks like it's traveled with you for years, designed by the boutique's owner.

Say it like La Parisienne

"It's really a store like no other. It carries brands that can't be found anywhere else in Paris."

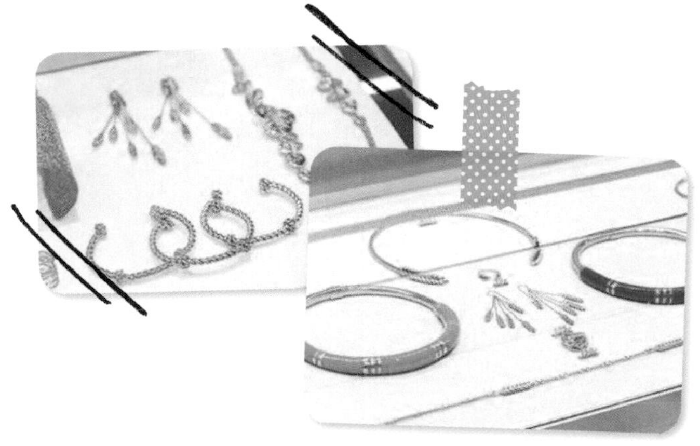

Aurélie Bidermann

55 bis, rue des Saints-Pères, VIe
Tel. +33 (0)1 45 48 43 14 — www.aureliebidermann.com

Why go? This designer's career has been fascinating to watch. She revolutionized the world of costume jewelry over the last ten years, with styles that never look outdated. Her Do Brasil line combines metallic chains and cotton threads and is one of the most imitated collections in the world. She now designs precious jewelry collections as well.

The must-have There are plenty of must-haves at Aurélie's. Buy whatever you like—perhaps a bracelet from the Serpent collection. The main thing is to keep collecting.

Say it like La Parisienne

"I always run into Aurélie at Ralph's (173, blvd Saint-Germain, VIe), Ralph Lauren's restaurant. It seems to be her lunch spot."

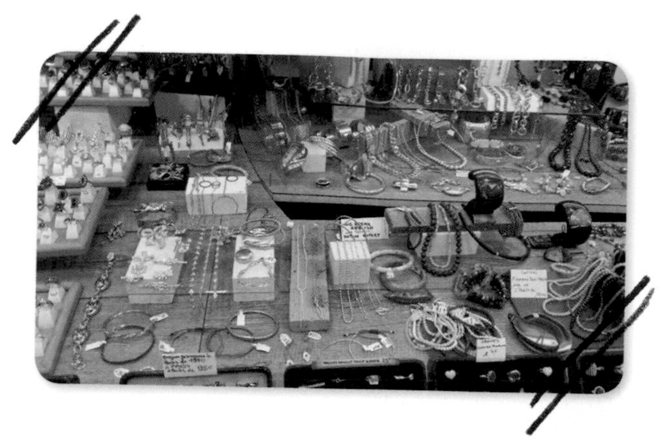

Monic

14, rue de l'Ancienne-Comédie, VIe
Tel. +33 (0)1 43 25 36 61
and 5, rue des Francs-Bourgeois, IVe
Tel. +33 (0)1 42 72 39 15

Why go? This boutique stocks thousands of jewelry items—every kind imaginable. But when I go to Monic's, I usually ask her to work on pieces of mine that need to be fixed or have gone out of style. She can completely transform them, thinking up ways to repurpose a pendant that I couldn't find any use for, or turning three gold baptismal medallions into a simply elegant bracelet. She has the magic touch.

→ **The must-have** Anything she creates for you from those two tarnished old rings that are languishing in your drawer.

Say it like La Parisienne

"Don't give this address away to just anybody. I'd hate to have to wait weeks for Monic to get around to melting down my old gold jewelry."

Curiosités

26–28, rue des Grands-Augustins, VIe
Tel. +33 (0)1 46 33 09 63

Why go? I like to visit this antique jewelry shop with my friend, the actress Sandrine Kiberlain. We're greeted by excited shouts of recognition as soon as we cross the threshold. The prices are very fair, and the owner is charming. But keep this secret address to yourself!

The must-have Intaglios, which are gemstones with designs engraved or carved into their surface. It's like owning a museum piece.

Say it like La Parisienne

"This ring's been in my family for generations."

RUE DU FOUR
APRIATI

Apriati

54, rue du Four, VIe
Tel. +33 (0)1 42 22 15 42 — www.apriati.com

Why go? It's an addiction. Once you start buying jewelry at Apriati, you crave it like a drug. Try on one of their bracelets if you want to feel like you're vacationing on Mykonos even if it's the middle of January. Prices run the gamut and every design is unique. I'm a collector, especially of her bracelets. But since I've only got two arms, I'll have to stop at some point. And these pieces have the prettiest clasps you've ever seen.

The must-have It's difficult to choose, but the 7 Cords bracelet may be my favorite. You select the color and clasp, along with a charm. It makes the perfect gift.

Say it like La Parisienne

"I've got the salesman Arthur's cell phone number in case you ever need it."

Pommade
Concrète
UNIVERSELLE BULY
Huiles

Buly 1803

6, rue Bonaparte, VIe
Tel. +33 (0)1 43 29 02 50 — www.buly1803.com

Why go? If only to admire the result of the owners' hard work to revive this venerable brand. It was purchased by artistic director Ramdane Touhami and his wife Victoire de Taillac. Of course, the brand has a long history, but every detail has been carefully rethought. You get the impression that the shop has been in business forever, despite its many years of slumber. Even its ceramic tile work has an old-fashioned, traditional feel.

→ **The must-have** Users all recommend Buly 1803 beauty products (creams, perfume oils, soaps, etc.) and its line of incense. I love them, too, but I go mainly for the Japanese makeup brushes.

Say it like La Parisienne

"You're immersed in a literary past the second you enter the shop. As you'd expect: the perfumer Jean-Vincent Buly was an inspiration for Honoré de Balzac's Human Comedy. *Today, Victoire, as* vendeuse *in a white-collared shirt and black sweater, looks every bit the part of a romantic heroine."*

Le Petit Souk

17, rue Vavin, VIe
Tel. +33 (0)1 42 02 23 71 — www.lepetitsouk.fr

Why go? If you're in the market for a newborn gift, you should check this place out for clothes and lots of other items that are fun and not too cutesy. You'll find a nightlight shaped like a bunny and little sleep sacks in adorable fabrics. The shop also carries decorative accessories and stationery—remember, you never have too many notebooks!

The must-have I once impulsively ordered a baby blanket with neon-colored roses from their website, as if I needed it desperately. I never found a use for it, but it's *so* pretty.

Say it like La Parisienne

"I go there to buy baby gifts, but I always leave with something for myself. It's where I found that wicker basket I take to the beach."

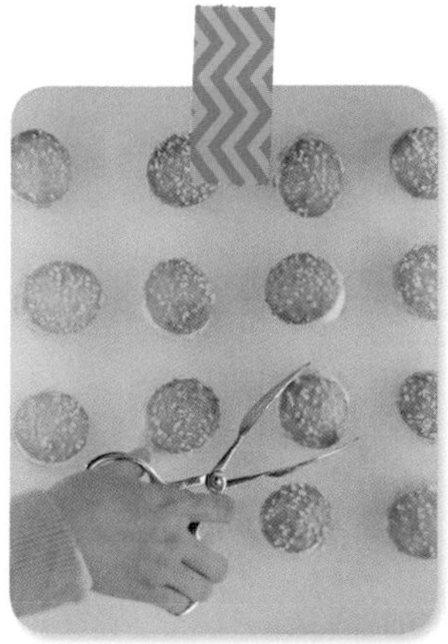

La Tarte Tropézienne

3, rue de Montfaucon, VIe
Tel. +33 (0)1 43 29 09 81 — www.latartetropezienne.fr

Why go? If you haven't experienced this cream-filled brioche, it's time. For years, you could only get it in Saint-Tropez, but now it's available in Paris. I'm delighted! I was born in the South of France and always love to go back there—especially to buy sandals from Rondini (www.rondini.fr), the other local specialty you absolutely have to try.

The must-have The *tarte tropézienne*, of course. My personal favorite is the *Baby Trop'* (a bite-size version of the *tarte tropézienne*). It's almost like a diet plan.

Say it like La Parisienne

"They say pâtissier Alexandre Micka named this confection after Brigitte Bardot. Remember Roger Vadim's film And God Created Pastry?"

Le Bon Saint Pourçain

10 bis, rue Servandoni, VIe
Tel. +33 (0)1 42 01 78 24

Why go? It's always been one of my favorite restaurants—an utterly Parisian spot that evokes the quintessence of the city. It's been bought by David Lanher, the genial restaurateur behind Racines (that I wrote about in *Parisian Chic*), Caffè Stern, and Noglu (a gluten-free restaurant and *épicerie*). The restaurant's had a fresh new makeover, and you'll fall in love with Mathieu Techer's cuisine.

→ **What to order?** The legendary *poireaux vinaigrette* (leeks in vinaigrette). Or the chicken, which is always beautifully prepared. And the dark chocolate mousse—unforgettable.

Say it like La Parisienne

"That man with the glasses who took our order—wasn't he a waiter at Café de Flore?"

Aux Prés

27, rue du Dragon, VIe
Tel. +33 (0)1 45 48 29 68 — www.restaurantauxpres.com

Why go? Because Cyril Lignac is one of the most talented and engaging chefs who has ever moved up to Paris from the Aveyron. His places (three restaurants in Paris and two pâtisseries) are just like their owner: very attractive indeed. He moved into the space formerly occupied by Claude Sainlouis's meat restaurant with its cult following, and he covered the room with wallpaper he found in the basement. As you'd expect, the décor radiates vintage chic.

→ **What to order?** Cyril's Black Angus burger with *frites*, mayonnaise, and curry honey is the best in Paris. And his salted caramel éclair is a killer dessert.

Say it like La Parisienne

"To take a bit of Cyril home with me, I buy his scented candles on www.cyrillignac.com."

Luisa Maria

12, rue Monsieur-le-Prince, VI[e]
Tel. +33 (0)1 43 29 62 49

Why go? Let's be clear: it's the best pizzeria in Paris. What's more, its little terrace is lovely in the summer, and it's even heated on cool autumn days. Naturally, the place is usually packed. If you happen to be on the right bank, you can meet your friends at the owners' other location, Maria Luisa (2, rue Marie-et-Louise, X[e]).

What to order? The pizza *du jour* is always a good choice. I still remember one that featured four varieties of tomato—it was delicious.

Say it like La Parisienne

"The owners are Neapolitan, so it's no surprise that they are pizza maestros. Like when a native of Alsace opens a restaurant that specializes in sauerkraut."

Café Trama

83, rue du Cherche-Midi, VIe
Tel. +33 (0)1 45 48 33 71

Why go? I first tried this place because my friend Domino lives next door. But I go back for the restaurant's appealing bistro atmosphere—a very Parisian blend of vintage 1950s and contemporary styles. It also offers extremely good traditional French cuisine with specialties like *rillettes de porc, boeuf tartare*, and *pot au feu*. And here's a plus: you can bring along your children when you eat here—they're perfectly welcome.

What to order? The *croque-monsier Poujauran au sel de truffe* (croque-monsieur with truffle salt).

Say it like La Parisienne

"The owner is Marion—Marion Trama."

Maison du Kashmir

8, rue Sainte-Beuve, VIe
Tel. +33 (0)1 45 48 66 06 — www.maisondukashmir.fr

59

Why go? When you're hankering for a good curry. Don't forget that Kashmir is first and foremost a region of India, not just a source for soft sweaters. The kitchen turns out dependable basics: samosas, Madras chicken, cheese-stuffed naans, and lamb prepared with coconut milk.

→ **What to order?** Try the Chicken Tikka Masala, with a fruit lassi.

Say it like La Parisienne

"When pulling together a last-minute dinner with friends, I just order everything from Maison du Kashmir. They deliver all over Paris."

LE HIBOU

Le Hibou

16, carrefour de l'Odéon, VIe
Tel. +33 (0)1 43 54 96 91 — www.lehibouparis.fr

Why go? There aren't many outdoor terraces in this neighborhood. This one's well located at the carrefour de l'Odéon. Its décor is pretty (you get the impression someone's been antiquing in the flea markets). Blue is the predominant color, which somehow makes you feel like you're on vacation. It's the ideal spot before or after a film at the Odéon cinema, and it's even open on Sundays.

→ **What to order?** The *salade chinoise* is really good.

Say it like La Parisienne

"Don't you think it's got a New York feel with a Lower East Side buzz? But the owner's from the region of Aveyron in the south. He's the same guy who bought Sénéquier, that legendary café in Saint-Tropez."

Allard

41, rue Saint-André-des-Arts
(main entrance at 1, rue de l'Éperon), VIe
Tel. +33 (0)1 58 00 23 42 — www.restaurant-allard.fr

Why go? I bet nobody thought I'd mention Allard, but tourists reading this guide will be glad to hear about this throwback to the Paris of yesteryear. I wasn't around in 1932, but I don't think the setting has changed much. It's one of the city's last authentic bistros. Legendary chef Alain Ducasse has taken over the reins of this traditional spot.

→ **What to order?** *Œufs cocotte aux champignons, carré d'agneau, sole meunière, profiteroles, île flottante.* Everything on the menu is a traditional French specialty reinvented by Ducasse, who knows how to update the classics with respect.

Say it like La Parisienne

"These days the cuisine is by Ducasse, but it was Marthe Allard who was stirring the pot back in 1932. She was a Burgundian peasant who moved up to Paris with her old-time family recipes in hand."

62
63

Ines's all-time favorites

62 Sœur

Teen clothes that are just too cute

88, rue Bonaparte, VIe
Tel. +33 (0)1 46 34 19 33
www.soeur.fr

63 Marie-Hélène de Taillac

Indian-inspired jewelry that warms the heart

8, rue de Tournon, VIe
Tel. +33 (0)1 44 27 07 07
www.mariehelenedetaillac.com

64 Adelline

Jewelry pure and simple

54, rue Jacob, VIe
Tel. +33 (0)1 47 03 07 18
www.adelline.com

65 Attal Cordonnerie

A cobbler who makes marvelous sandals

122, rue d'Assas, VIe
Tel. +33 (0)1 46 34 52 33

66 Bread & Roses

The café with the creamiest cheesecake

62, rue Madame, VIe
Tel. +33 (0)1 42 22 06 06
www.breadandroses.fr

67 La Villa Madame

The most charming hotel in Paris

44, rue Madame, VIe
Tel. +33 (0)1 45 48 02 81
www.hotelvillamadameparis.com

68 L'Hôtel

The most discreet hotel in Paris

13, rue des Beaux-Arts, VIe
Tel. +33 (0)1 44 41 99 00
www.l-hotel.com

69 Café de Flore

The most Parisian of cafés

172, blvd Saint-Germain, VIe
Tel. +33 (0)1 45 48 55 26

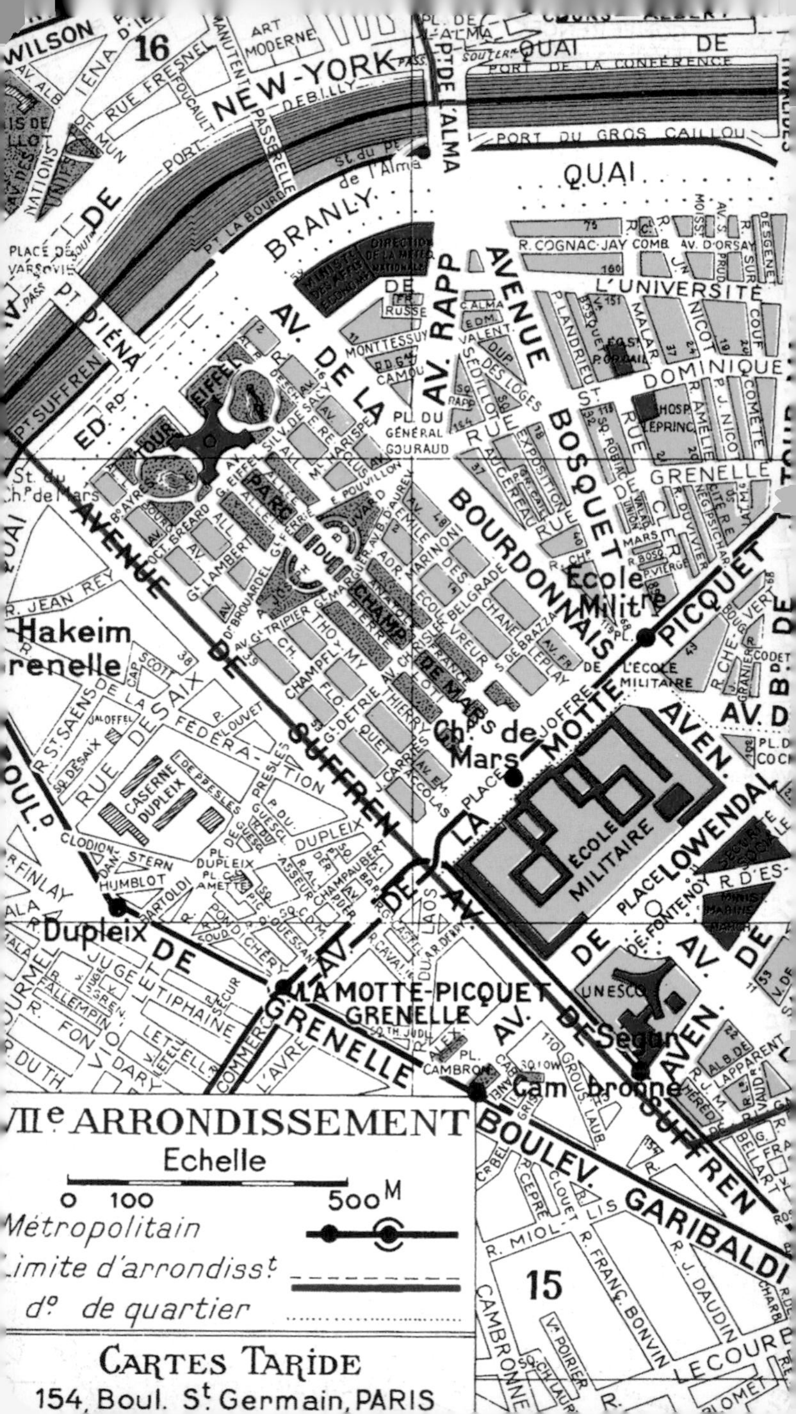
VIIe ARRONDISSEMENT
Echelle
0 100 500M
Métropolitain
Limite d'arrondisst
do de quartier
CARTES TARIDE
154, Boul. St Germain, PARIS
NEW-YORK
QUAI
BRANLY
AV. RAPP
AVENUE BOSQUET
BOURDONNAIS
AVENUE DE SUFFREN
PARC DU CHAMP DE MARS
Ch. de Mars
ÉCOLE MILITAIRE
Ecole Milit re
PLACE DE LA MOTTE-PICQUET
LA MOTTE-PICQUET GRENELLE
Dupleix
Cambronne
Ségur
UNESCO
BOULEV. GARIBALDI
AV. DE LOWENDAL
PLACE DE FONTENOY
Bir-Hakeim Grenelle
RUE DESAIX
CASERNE DUPLEIX
L'UNIVERSITÉ
DOMINIQUE
GRENELLE
PT D'IÉNA
PT SUFFREN
PT DE L'ALMA
16
15

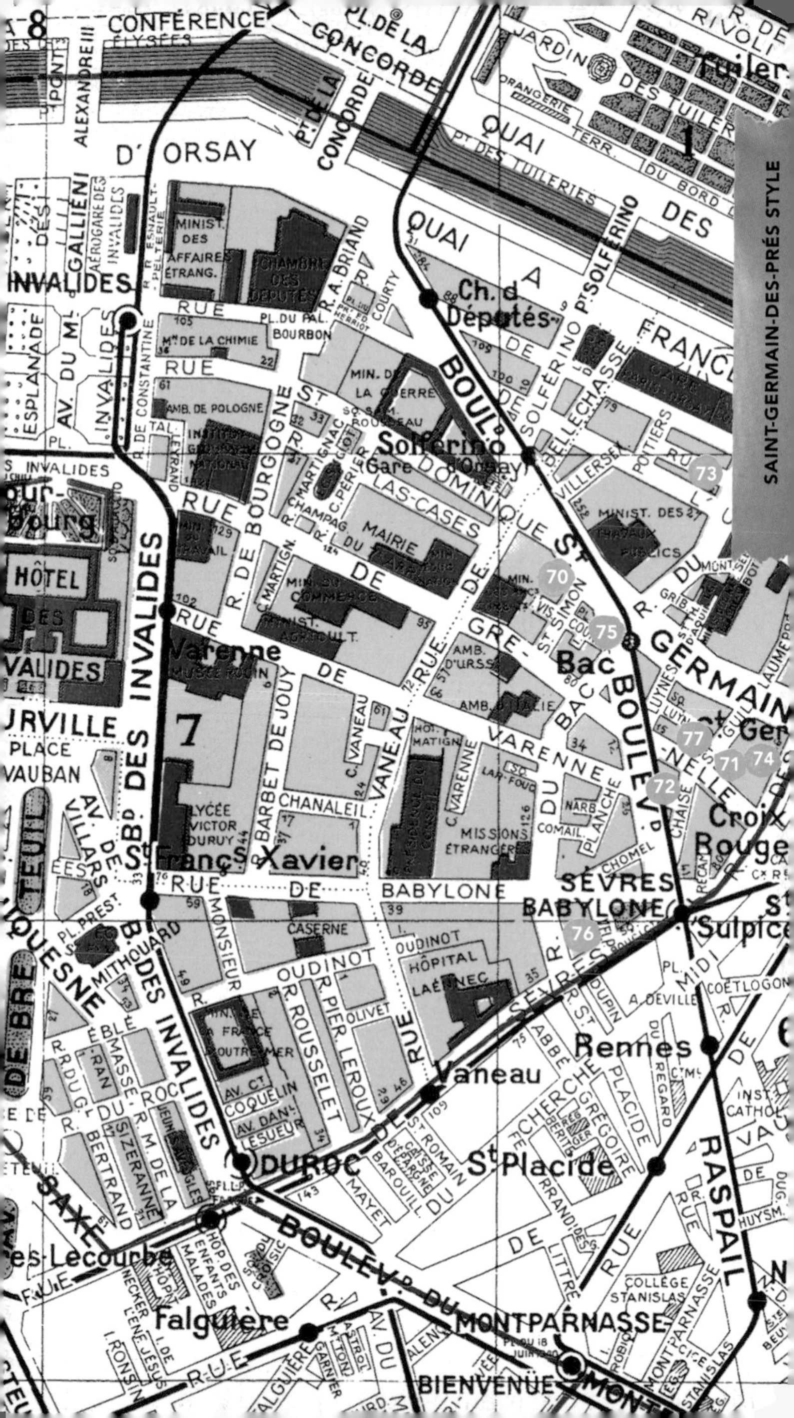
8
CONFÉRENCE
PL. DE LA CONCORDE
R. DE RIVOLI
JARDIN DES TUILERIES
ORANGERIE
Tuiler
1
PT DE LA CONCORDE
PONT ALEXANDRE III
QUAI D'ORSAY
QUAI
PT DES TUILERIES
DU BORD
PT SOLFÉRINO
QUAI A FRANCE
DES
AV. DU MAL GALLIÉNI
AÉROGARE DES INVALIDES
MINIST. DES AFFAIRES ÉTRANG.
CHAMBRE DES DÉPUTÉS
R. A. BRIAND
COURTY
INVALIDES
Ch. d Députés
ESPLANADE
INVALIDES
RUE
PL. DU PAL. BOURBON
Mre DE LA CHIMIE
R. DE CONSTANTINE
GARE
MIN. DE LA GUERRE
BOUL.D
DE
SOLFÉRINO
R. DE BELLECHASSE
AMB. DE POLOGNE
INSTITUT GÉOGRAPHIQUE NATIONAL
R. DE BOURGOGNE
ST
SQ. SAM. ROUSSEAU
Solférino (Gare d'Orsay)
DOMINIQUE
73
POITIERS
VILLERSEX.
MINIST. DES TRAVAUX PUBLICS
LAS-CASES
MAIRIE DU 7E ARR.
RUE
MIN. DU TRAVAIL
Bourg
HÔTEL DES INVALIDES
MIN. DU COMMERCE
MINIST. AGRICULT.
70
75
ST SIMON
R. DU
GERMAIN
Bac
GRE-
BAC
BOULEVD
MONTALEMBERT
BOULEVD DES INVALIDES
Varenne
MUSÉE RODIN
RUE DE VARENNE
AMB. D'U.R.S.S.
AMB. D'ITALIE
LUYNES
St Ger
77
71
74
72
NESLE
RVILLE
PLACE VAUBAN
7
R. BARBET DE JOUY
C. VANEAU
RUE VANEAU
HÔT. MATIGNON
PRÉSIDENCE DU CONSEIL
C. VARENNE
SQ. LAR-FOUC
MISSIONS ÉTRANGÈRES
R. DU BAC
NARB
COMAIL
PLANCHE
CHAISE
Croix Rouge
CHANALEIL
LYCÉE VICTOR DURUY
St Franc's Xavier
AV. DE VILLARS
RUE DE BABYLONE
CHOMEL
SÈVRES BABYLONE
St Sulpice
TEUIL
QUESNE
MITHOUARD
CASERNE
OUDINOT
HÔPITAL LAENNEC
76
R. DE SÈVRES
R. DU MIDI
COETLOGON
A. DEVILLE
RUE MONSIEUR
R. OUDINOT
R. PIER. LEROUX
R. ROUSSELET
OLIVET
DUPIN
Rennes
MIN. DE LA FRANCE D'OUTREMER
ABBÉ
DU REGARD
INST. CATHOL.
R. ÉBLÉ
R. MASSE
AV. CT. COQUELIN
AV. DANL LESUEUR
RUE
Vaneau
CHERCHE
PLACIDE
GRÉGOIRE
R. DU ROC
R. M. DE LA
SIZERANNE
BERTRAND
DUROC
BAROUILL
MAYET
ST ROMAIN
CAISSE D'ÉPARGNE
St Placide
RASPAIL
HUYSM.
SAXE
HOP. DES ENFANTS MALADES
BOULEVD DU MONTPARNASSE
DE
LITTRÉ
RUE
COLLÈGE STANISLAS
Es-Lecourbe
RUE
Falguière
R.
AV. DU
NECKER
PL. DU 18 JUIN 1940
BIENVENÜE
MONT
STANISLAS

Simone

1, rue de Saint-Simon, VIIe
Tel. +33 (0)1 42 22 81 40 — www.simoneruesaintsimon.com

Why go? When I realized that I completely forgot to include this fashion destination in my book *Parisian Chic,* I was a mess, and nibbed away at my nails until they completely disappeared. So, I'm delighted to be able to talk about it in this city guide, because it's a hidden treasure totally off the beaten path. You wouldn't happen upon it if you weren't told where to look. The owner—who's not named Simone, by the way—is a savvy buyer who seeks out labels you won't find anywhere else. She also has a talent for selecting flattering looks. It's a stylish, upbeat place.

The must-have Laura Urbinati's knits. I absolutely love them. Actually, everything here is a must-have. There's new stock arriving all the time, so you should visit often.

Say it like La Parisienne

"They always have the most interesting colors here. So even if I buy something that doesn't suit me, it certainly brightens up my closet."

24
INES DE LA FRESSANGE
PARIS

Ines de la Fressange Paris

24, rue de Grenelle, VIIe
Tel. +33 (0)1 45 48 19 06 — www.inesdelafressange.fr

Why go? If I could mention only one boutique in this guide, this would be it! Not because you'll find my own designs here, but because this is the place to buy anything from a chic leather bag to a handy toothbrush holder. Think of it as a cross between a fantasy department store and a sundries emporium.

The must-have It's hard to decide. I'm tempted to say "Everything" ;-). There are fashion options (some of the styles are in very limited editions), as well as jewelry, shoes, sunglasses, notebooks, and lots of home décor items. Even brooms! One thing's for sure—people come from all over Paris for the olive oil we sell.

Say it like La Parisienne

"I went in to get a pencil sharpener and ended up ordering a full-length gown from the design studio."

Noro

4–6, rue de Varenne, VIIe
Tel. +33 (0)1 45 49 19 88 — www.noroparis.com

Why go? There are times when you want famous designer names. But sometimes you're looking for smaller, less well-known brands like Noro, whose motto is "Poetic, discreet but precious." They have clothing for women, children, and infants, and they stock other brands as well, including an ethno-chic jacket by Pero.

→ **The must-have** All the cotton blouses from Noro. And the wool cardigans: basic, but essential.

Say it like La Parisienne

"Come on, let's go to Ines de la Fressange next. It's just up the street."

Romain Réa

26, rue du Bac, VIIe
Tel. +33 (0)1 42 61 43 44 — www.romainrea.com

Why go? Because there are times when you have to give your guy a gift. And men can never have too many watches. Romain Réa is a highly respected watch expert (he works for the auction house Artcurial). You'll always find rarities in his shop—antique treasures that men really love. All the best brands are represented here, from Rolex and Jaeger-Lecoultre to Patek Philippe, Audemars Piguet, and Bell & Ross.

→ **The must-have** A watch that can't be found anywhere but Romain Réa's boutique is the obvious must-have.

Say it like La Parisienne

"Did you know that Romain Réa was Robert de Niro's 'wrist costumier*'? He advised the actor on which watch should be worn for each role."*

StONE
PARIS

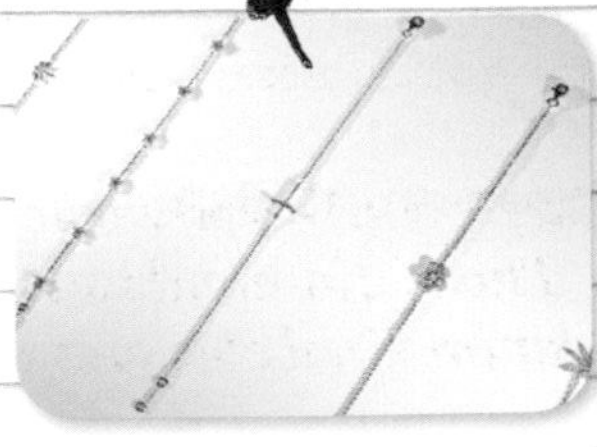

Stone Paris

60, rue des Saints-Pères, VIIe
Tel. +33 (0)1 42 22 24 24 — www.stoneparis.com

74

Why go? If one of my (well-off) readers would like to give me a nice diamond bracelet, I'll simplify your life and say that all you need to do is visit Stone. And if your fiancé wants to give you a real rock, you can be sure it won't be overly flashy if he buys it here. Designer Marie Poniatowski often works with the retailer Bonpoint to make jewelry appropriate for children.

→ **The must-have** All those elegant bracelets set with little diamonds. And everything else in the store.

Say it like La Parisienne

"These diamonds should be worn discreetly with denim. Cool chic guaranteed."

Lao Tseu

209, blvd Saint-Germain, VIIe
Tel. +33 (0)1 45 48 30 06

Why go? My friend George Kiejman, the attorney, claims this is the best Chinese restaurant in Paris. I should note, however, that his office is just around the corner. By the way, did you know that in Paris everyone has the best bakery at the end of their street?

What to order? Select from the menu of steamed specialties. It's reasonably priced and very good.

Say it like La Parisienne

"This is a regular haunt for editors. Budding writers would be better off dining here than sending in their manuscript."

Ines's all-time favorites

76 Le Bon Marché

The most exclusive department store collections

24, rue de Sèvres, VIIe
Tel. +33 (0)1 44 39 80 00
www.lebonmarche.com

77 Emmanuelle Zysman

Delightful jewelry

33, rue de Grenelle, VIIe
Tel. +33 (0)1 42 22 05 57
www.emmanuellezysman.fr

VIIIe ARRONDISSEMENT

Chic near the Champs-Élysées

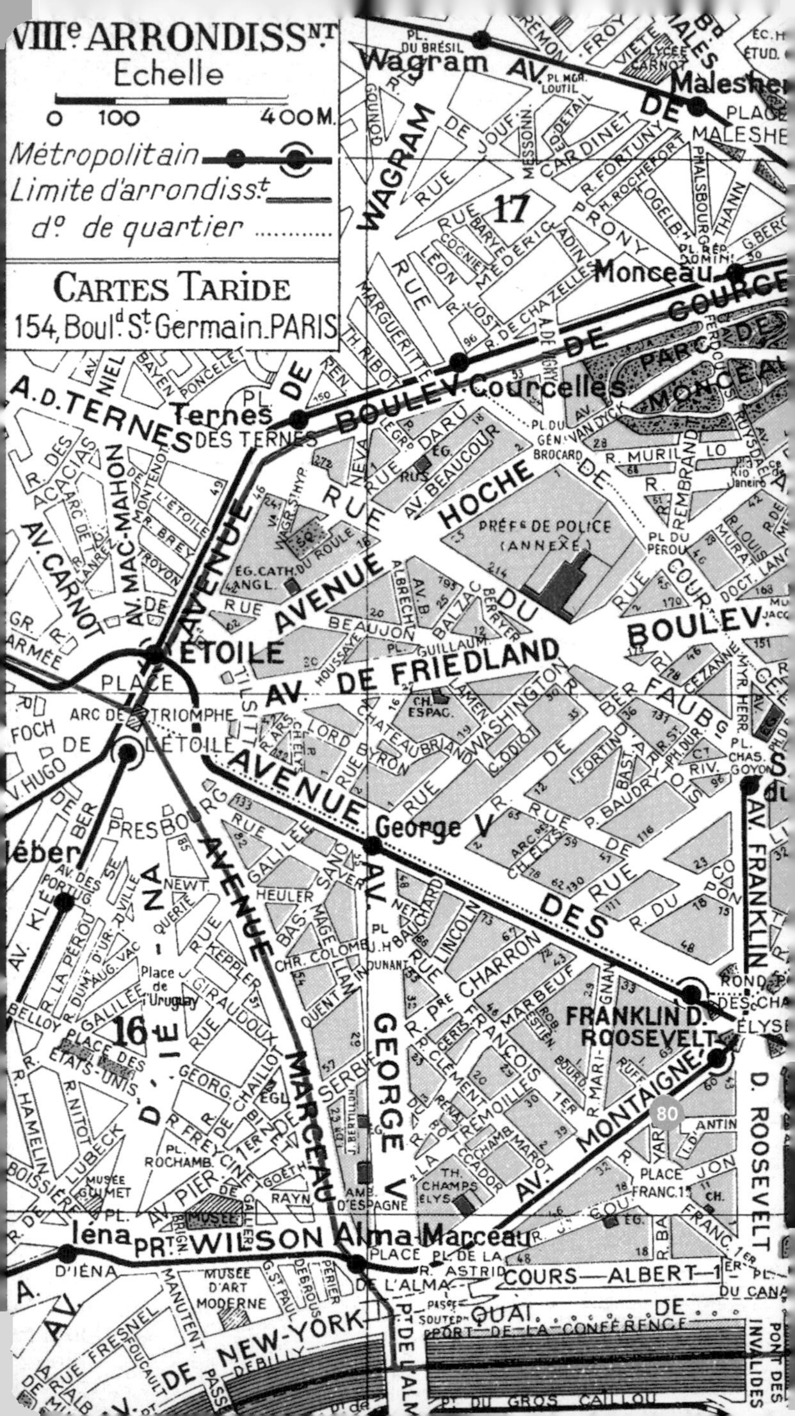
VIIIe ARRONDISSNT.
Echelle
0 100 400M.
Métropolitain
Limite d'arrondisst
do de quartier
CARTES TARIDE
154, Bould St Germain PARIS
Wagram
AV. DE WAGRAM
BD MALESHERBES
Malesherbes
PL. DU BRÉSIL
LYCÉE CARNOT
PLACE MALESHERBES
R. DE PRONY
RUE DE JOUFFROY
RUE CARDINET
R. FORTUNY
R. ROCHEFORT
PHALSBOURG
THANN
17
Monceau
BD DE COURCELLES
PARC DE MONCEAU
Courcelles
Ternes
PL. DES TERNES
A.D. TERNES
AV. NIEL
PONCELET
R. DES ACACIAS
AV. CARNOT
AV. MAC-MAHON
AVENUE DE WAGRAM
AVENUE HOCHE
RUE DARU
AV. BEAUCOUR
PRÉFre DE POLICE (ANNEXE)
RUE DU FAUBG ST-HONORÉ
BOULEV. HAUSSMANN
R. MURILLO
R. REMBRANDT
PL. DU PÉROU
R. DE COURCELLES
ÉG. CATH. ANGL.
AV. DE FRIEDLAND
RUE BEAUJON
AV. BALZAC
BERRYER
ÉTOILE
PLACE DE L'ÉTOILE
ARC DE TRIOMPHE
AV. FOCH
AV. V. HUGO
AVENUE DES CHAMPS-ÉLYSÉES
R. WASHINGTON
RUE LORD BYRON
CHATEAUBRIAND
R. DE BERRI
George V
RUE DE PRESBOURG
AVENUE MARCEAU
AV. KLÉBER
Kléber
R. GALILÉE
R. LA PÉROUSE
Place de l'Uruguay
16
PLACE DES ÉTATS-UNIS
AV. D'IÉNA
R. HAMELIN
RUE LINCOLN
R. PRE CHARRON
R. MARBEUF
R. FRANÇOIS 1ER
FRANKLIN D. ROOSEVELT
AV. FRANKLIN D. ROOSEVELT
AV. MONTAIGNE
AV. GEORGE V
RUE DE LA TRÉMOILLE
PL. D'ESPAGNE
TH. CHAMPS ÉLYS.
PLACE FRANC. 1ER
RD PT DES CHAMPS ÉLYSÉES
MUSÉE GUIMET
léna
AV. PRT WILSON
Alma-Marceau
PLACE DE L'ALMA
COURS ALBERT 1ER
MUSÉE D'ART MODERNE
AV. DE NEW-YORK
QUAI DE LA CONFÉRENCE
PONT DES INVALIDES
PT DU GROS CAILLOU

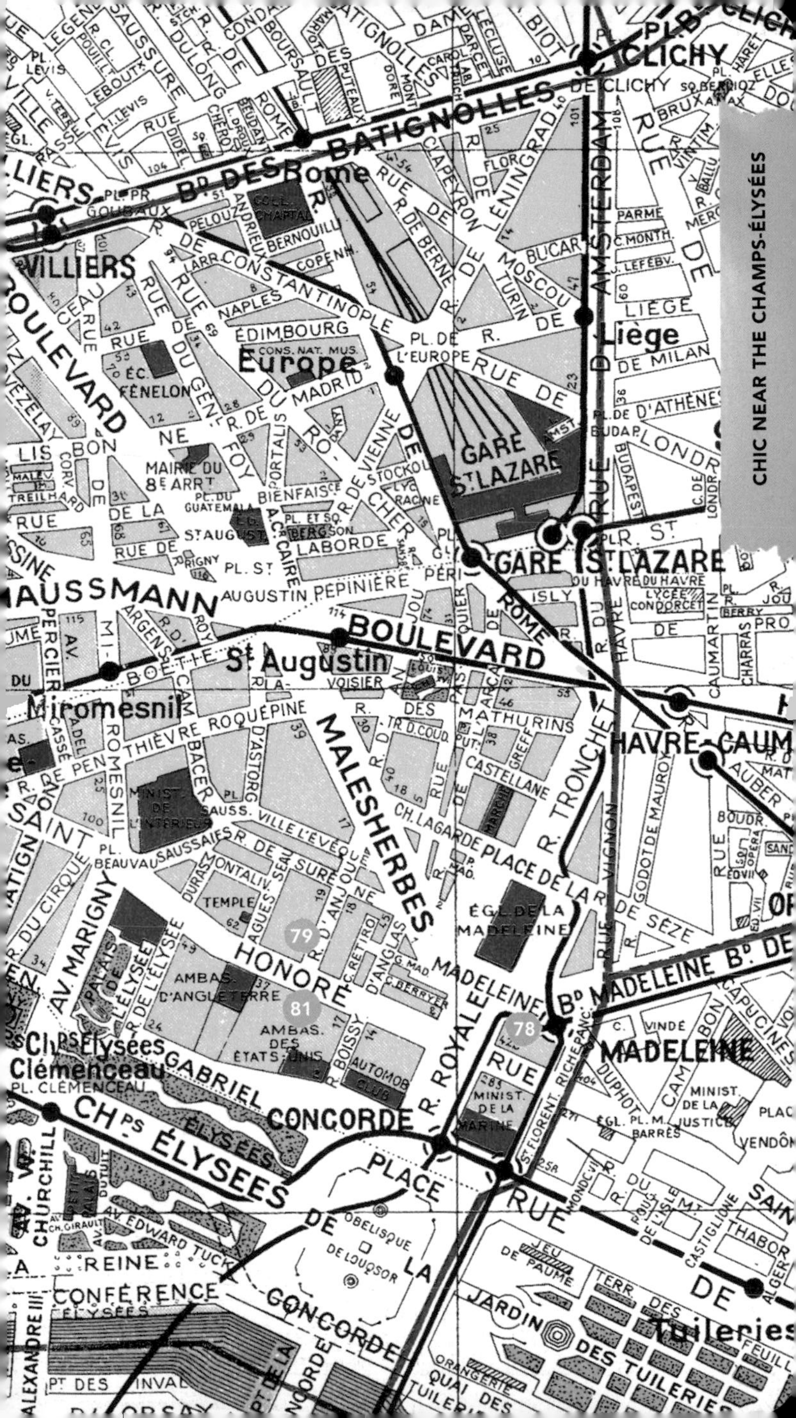
CLICHY
PL. DE CLICHY
Bd DES BATIGNOLLES
Rome
VILLIERS
BOULEVARD
RUE DE CONSTANTINOPLE
RUE DE NAPLES
ÉDIMBOURG
Europe
PL. DE L'EUROPE
RUE DE MADRID
RUE DE ROME
RUE DE LÉNINGRAD
RUE DE MOSCOU
RUE DE TURIN
RUE DE BERNE
RUE D'AMSTERDAM
Liège
RUE DE LIÈGE
DE MILAN
PL. DE D'ATHÈNES
LONDRES
BUDAPEST
GARE St LAZARE
GARE St LAZARE
COLL. CHAPTAL
BERNOUILLI
COPENH.
ÉC. FÉNELON
MAIRIE DU 8e ARRT
PL. DU GUATEMALA
ÉG. St AUGUST.
PL. St AUGUSTIN
LABORDE
PÉPINIÈRE
ROCHER
STOCKOLM
LYC. RACINE
HAUSSMANN
BOULEVARD
St Augustin
Miromesnil
LA BOÉTIE
VOISIER
DES MATHURINS
ISLY
LYCÉE CONDORCET
DU HAVRE
CAUMARTIN
HAVRE-CAUMARTIN
R. TRONCHET
R. DE PENTHIÈVRE
ROQUÉPINE
MALESHERBES
MINIST. DE L'INTÉRIEUR
PL. BEAUVAU
SAUSSAIES
R. DE SURÈNE
CH. LAGARDE
PLACE DE LA MADELEINE
ÉGL. DE LA MADELEINE
R. DE SÈZE
VIGNON
GODOT DE MAUROY
AUBER
TEMPLE
HONORÉ
AMBAS. D'ANGLETERRE
AMBAS. DES ÉTATS-UNIS
AUTOMOB. CLUB
R. BOISSY D'ANGLAS
R. ROYALE
Bd MADELEINE
MADELEINE
MINIST. DE LA MARINE
MINIST. DE LA JUSTICE
R. DUPHOT
CAMBON
CAPUCINES
Bd DES
VENDÔME
AV. MARIGNY
PALAIS DE L'ÉLYSÉE
R. DU CIRQUE
Ch ps Élysées Clémenceau
PL. CLÉMENCEAU
GABRIEL
CONCORDE
CH ps ÉLYSÉES
PLACE DE LA CONCORDE
OBÉLISQUE DE LOUQSOR
RUE DE RIVOLI
JEU DE PAUME
JARDIN DES TUILERIES
TERR. DES FEUILL.
Tuileries
ORANGERIE
QUAI DES TUILERIES
CASTIGLIONE
THABOR
AV. W. CHURCHILL
PETIT PALAIS
AV. EDWARD TUCK
REINE
CONFÉRENCE
ALEXANDRE III
PT DES INVAL
PT DE LA CONCORDE
79
81
78

Margaret Howell

6, place de la Madeleine, VIIIe
Tel. +33 (0)1 42 61 90 00 — www.margarethowell.fr

Why go? This brand is the embodiment of classic-chic style. You'll find everything you need, whether you're after a sleek refined look or want to tone down a piece that's a bit over the top. You could say that the clothing here is somewhat androgynous: navy blue trousers, a simple sky-blue shirt, a cream-colored turtleneck sweater. Described like this, it may not sound that fun, but this really is an address you should know about. It's not a place for bargain prices, though!

→ **The must-have** An oversize cashmere sweater or a knit sailor top.

Say it like La Parisienne

"I hear that Phoebe Philo, Céline's artistic director, wears pieces by Margaret Howell."

Philippine Janssens

3–5, rue d'Anjou, VIIIe
Tel. +33 (0)1 42 65 43 90 — www.philippinejanssens.com
By appointment only

Why go? Don't tell me you've found the perfect pair of trousers—there's really no such thing. Unless of course you go to Philippine's. It's the first shop that's dedicated entirely to creating tailor-made trousers for women. She sews the pants exclusively for you, so obviously they'll suit you perfectly.

→ **The must-have** Your very own trousers.

Say it like La Parisienne

"The 'perfect size' doesn't exist. I know plenty of fashion models who have their trousers custom-made by Philippine."

Hanawa

26, rue Bayard, VIIIe
Tel. +33 (0)1 56 62 70 70 — www.hanawa.fr

Why go? To mingle with *le Tout-Paris* of the media, film, and music worlds. And *le Tout-Hollywood* also gets the appeal of this spot. I go mostly for their beef with ginger. Hanawa is a landmark on rue Bayard, just as Christian Dior's couture salon is a shrine on nearby avenue Montaigne. This restaurant has the reputation for serving the best Japanese food in Europe.

What to order? If you order a bento box, you can enjoy your entire meal as a single course.

Say it like La Parisienne

"Did you say hello to Demi Moore? She's sitting in the back with Salma Hayek."

Ines's all-time favorites

81 Roger Vivier

The luxury flagship store where I have my office

29, rue du Faubourg-Saint-Honoré, VIIIe
Tel. +33 (0)1 53 43 00 85
www.rogervivier.com

IXe, X^{e}, XIe & XIIe
ARRONDISSEMENTS

The Bobo Attitude

Bd DE
PLACE BLANCHE
Blanche
CLICHY
PLACE PIGALLE
PIGAL
ABBESSES
18
PL. DE CLICHY
CLICHY
LYCÉE J. FERRY
R. BIOT
R. LEPIC
R. COUTOU
PL. SQ. BERLIOZ
AD. MAX
ELLES
BRUXELLES
VINTIMILLE
CALAIS
RUE DE DOUAI
RUE FONTAINE
RUE PIGALLE
MANSART
DUPERRÉ
FROMENTIN
R. GERM. PILON
R. CHAPTAL
C. CHAPT.
ESCUDIER
MONCEY
HENNER
C. PIGALLE
R. VR.
R. H. MONNIER
NAVARIN
CLAUZEL
MASSÉ
R. DE LA BRUYÈRE
SQ. LA BRUYÈRE
TH. PIGALLE
R. TOUR DES DAMES
R. LA ROCHEFOUCAULD
ND DE LORETTE
PL. ST GEORGES
St Ge
9
R. D'AUMALE
SQ. D'ORLÉANS
RUE ST LAZARE
BALLU
R. CL. MERCIER
RUE BLANCHE
RUE DE CLICHY
PARME
C. MONTH.
LEFEBVRE
BUCAR.
MOSCOU
TURIN
LÉNINGRAD
LIÈGE
Liège
RUE D'AMSTERDAM
R. DE MILAN
D'ATHÈNES
PL. DE BUDAPEST
LONDRES
APOLLO
CASINO DE PARIS
POMMIERS
TRINITÉ
ÉGL.
SQ.
PL. EST.NE D'ORVES
Trinité d'Est. d'Orves
N-D de Lorette
DE CHATEAUDUN
R. DE LA CHAUSSÉE D'ANTIN
DE LA VICTOIRE
TAITBOUT
ST GEORGES
PL. DU HAVRE
GARE ST LAZARE
St LAZARE
LYCÉE CONDORCET
STL. D'ANTIN
ROME
L'ISLY
R. DU HAVRE
R. CAUMARTIN
R. JOUBERT
G. BERRY
PROVENCE
CHARRAS
MOGADOR
DUCOQ
AV. DE PROV.
CITÉ D'ANTIN
RUE DE PROVENCE
PILLET
LAFFITTE
BD HAUSSMANN
HAUSSMANN
HAVRE - CAUMARTIN
CHÉE D'ANTIN
PL. AD. WILL
GOUDIN
MATHURINS
R. TRONCHET
GREFF.
CASTELLANE
ARCADE
VIGNON
GODOT DE MAUROY
AUBER
SCRIBE
PL. GLUCK
PL. DIAGHILEV
OPÉRA
HALÉVY
MEYERBEER
R. DU HELDER
ITALIENS
RICH
BOUDR.
PL. CH. GARNIER
TH. CAUMART.
S. OPÉRA L. JOUVET
SAND.
ÉD. VII
PL. DE L'OPÉRA
OPÉRA
Bd DES ITA
PLACE DE LA MADELEINE
R. DE SÈZE
OLYMPIA
Bd MADELEINE
Bd DES CAPUCINES
CHOISEUL
MONT
MARIVAUX
HANOVRE
4 Sept
R. DU 4 SEPTEMBRE
MÉNARS
GRETRY
BOÏEL.
R. DAUNOU
R. DE LA PAIX
CAPUCINES
VOLNEY
CITÉ VINDÉ
MADELEINE
1
ST HONORÉ
DUPHOT
CAMBON
R. DE LA
LOUIS
NOUVEAU
D. CASANOVA
AV. DE L'OPÉRA
PT MAHON
MICHODIÈRE
GAILL.
MONSIGNY
R. DE CHOISEUL
STE ANNE
GRAMONT
ST AUGUSTIN
LOUVOIS

THE BOBO ATTITUDE

IXe ARRONDISSE

Echelle

0 100

Métropolitain

Limite d'arrondisst

d° de quartier

CARTES TARIDE

154 Boul. St Germ

BOULD ROCHECHOUART

BARBÈS-ROCHECHT

Bd DE LA CHAPELLE

BOULd Anvers

LYCÉE JACQUES DECOUR

AV. TRUDAINE

RUE CONDORCET

R. DE LA TOUR D'AUVERGNE

RUE DE MAUBEUGE

HÔPITAL LARIBOISIÈRE

GARE DU NORD

BOULEVd DE MAGENTA

R. DE DUNKERQUE

Poissonre

RUE DE CHABROL

LAMARTINE

LA FAYETTE

Cadet

le Peletier

GR. ORIENT DE FRANCE

FOLIES BERG.

RUE RICHER

RUE DU FAUBG POISSONNIÈRE

RUE DE PARADIS

R. DES PET. ÉCURIES

RUE D'HAUTEVILLE

10

MAIRIE DU 9e ARR.

RUE BERGÈRE

RUE DU FAUBG MONTMARTRE

B. MONTMtre

B. POISSONNIÈRE

Monttre

Bnne Nouv.

RUE D'ENGHIEN

RUE ÉCHIQUIER

R. DES JEUNEURS

R. DU SENTIER

CROISSANT

Sentier

Bourse

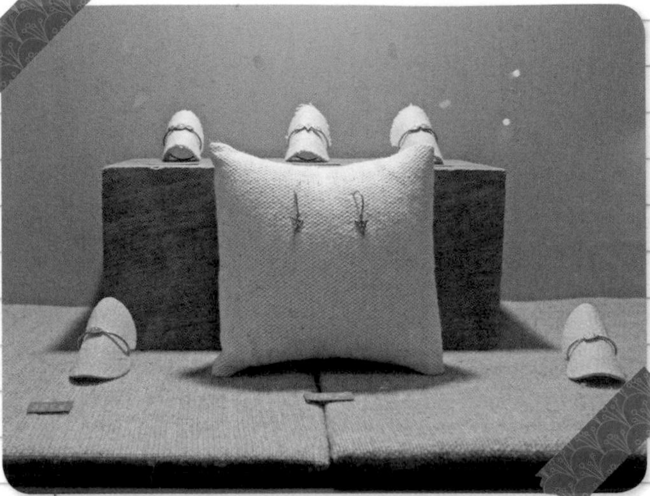

Myrtille Beck

30, rue Henry-Monnier, IXe
Tel. +33 (0)1 40 23 99 84 — www.myrtillebeck.com

Why go? This is a pretty little shop offering jewelry that somehow melds poetic and rock sensibilities. You'll find yourself thinking "I've got to have that!" whenever you see one of Myrtille Beck's designs. You can also visit her workshop to have your jewelry revamped or repaired.

The must-have Why not wear rings from the Amour Céleste collection right away? Even if you're not planning to get married!

Say it like La Parisienne

"This is awful! Myrtille Beck has an online store. I'd better cancel my internet account, or I'll be up all night ordering jewelry!"

Sept Cinq

54, rue Notre-Dame-de-Lorette, IXᵉ
Tel. +33 (0)9 83 55 05 95 — www.sept-cinq.com

Why go? All the designers represented in this concept store are Parisian. You'll find fashion, decorative accessories, *art de vivre* whimsies, cultural activities, and even a *salon de thé*. It's the quintessence of the city, flawlessly staged by two charming *Parisiennes*.

→ **The must-have** Ringo rings, a Charlie Watch, Season Paper note pads—everything is tempting.

Say it like La Parisienne

"Of course it wasn't listed in Parisian Chic. *The shop opened long after the book was published."*

Sugar Daze

20, rue Henry-Monnier, IXe
Tel. +33 (0)9 83 04 41 77 — www.sugardazecupcakes.com

Why go? You've heard it said that the cupcake craze is so over. Personally, I don't care about trends in cooking any more than I care about trends in fashion. The main thing is to have style, and the cupcake style still suits me fine. You can order birthday cakes here, too—stylish ones, naturally.

What to order? Cupcakes, obviously. But not only cupcakes; the brownies with sprinkles are worth gaining a few extra pounds.

Say it like La Parisienne

"This year, I'd like a leopard-print birthday cake from Sugar Daze."

FROMAGE
& CHARCUTERIE

Causses

55, rue Notre-Dame-de-Lorette, IXe
Tel. +33 (0)1 53 16 10 10 — www.causses.org

Why go? I wish there were more places like this in Paris. It reminds me of the New York specialty food store Dean & Deluca. Everything here is healthy, tasty, and simple. Their soups and sandwiches are outstanding.

What to order? Don't leave without picking up some treats from the grocery section. The products they sell here are incredible. Sometimes, some good cheese can make a great dinner.

Say it like La Parisienne
"It's in South Pigalle."

La Maison Mère

4, rue de Navarin, IXe
Tel. +33 (0)1 42 81 11 00 — www.lamaisonmere.fr

Why go? It's a really fun restaurant that features comfort food. White tiles, vintage furniture, hanging lamps with bowler hat shades—just relax and enjoy. It's the perfect place to take a break from shopping. And their Sunday brunch is terrific.

What to order? Try a cheeseburger, a bagel with smoked salmon, fish & chips, or maybe a slice of cheesecake. It's that kind of menu.

Say it like La Parisienne

"Among the cheese selections, the Comté from Jura is superb. So are their seasonal fruit platters."

Musée de la Vie Romantique

16, rue Chaptal, IXe
Tel. +33 (0)1 55 31 95 67

Why go? When it comes to museums, Paris offers plenty of options beyond the iconic Louvre. Check out this utterly charming little museum, where you almost expect to see George Sand and Chopin appear before your eyes.

Good to know The ground floor rooms display numerous pieces of furniture, sculpture, decorative objects, and jewelry that once belonged to George Sand.

Say it like La Parisienne

"Really? There are paintings to see inside? I spent my entire day in the garden—it's lovely here."

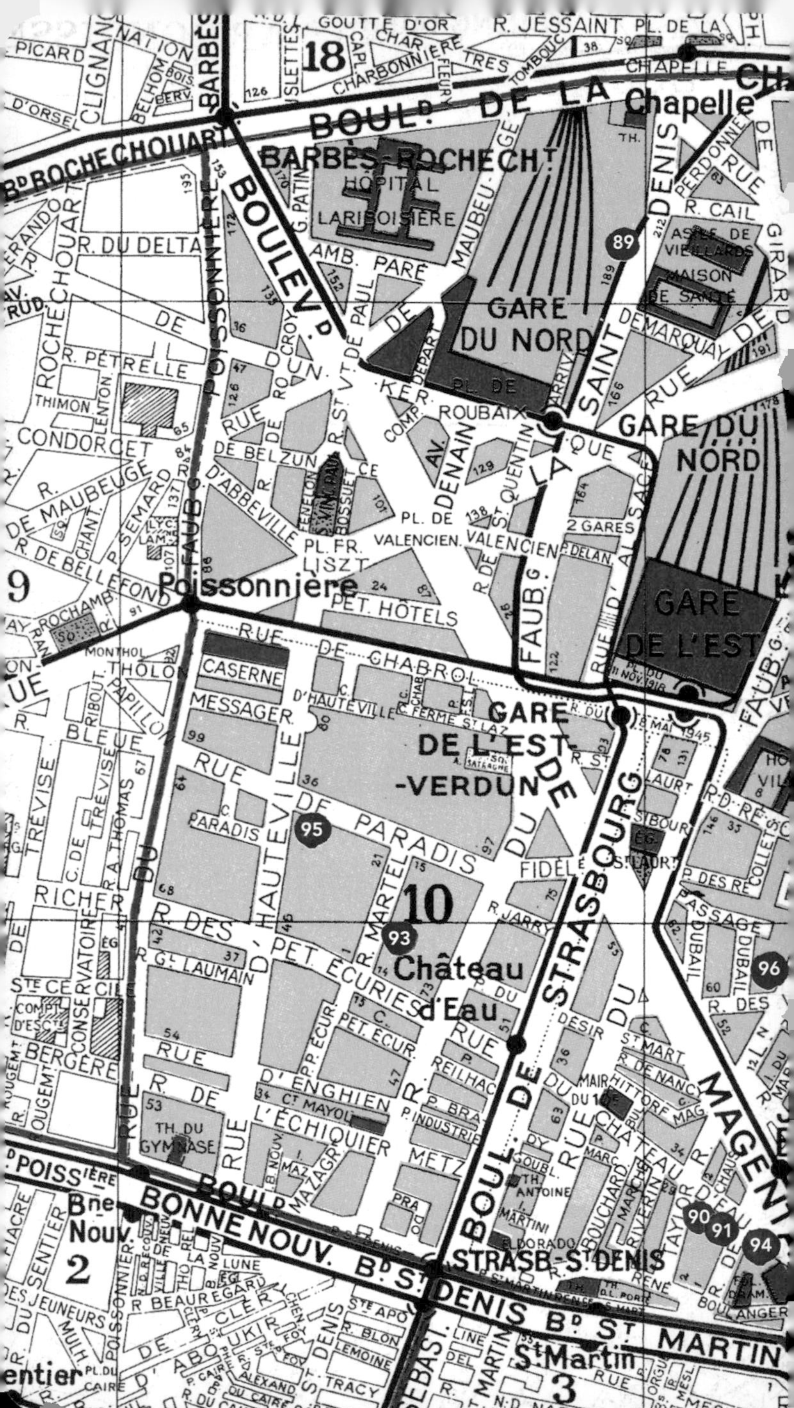

18
BOULD DE LA Chapelle
BD ROCHECHOUART
BARBÈS
BARBÈS-ROCHECHT
HÔPITAL LARIBOISIÈRE
R. DU DELTA
BOULEVD DE MAGENTA
GARE DU NORD
PL. DE ROUBAIX
GARE DU NORD
R. CAIL
ASILE DE VIEILLARDS
MAISON DE SANTÉ
RUE DEMARQUAY
RUE LA FAYETTE
RUE DE DUNKERQUE
R. PÉTRELLE
R. CONDORCET
R. DE MAUBEUGE
RUE DE BELZUNCE
R. D'ABBEVILLE
PL. FR. LISZT
PL. DE VALENCIEN.
R. DE ST QUENTIN
R. DES 2 GARES
FAUB G ST DENIS
9
Poissonnière
PET. HÔTELS
RUE DE CHABROL
CASERNE
GARE DE L'EST
GARE DE L'EST-VERDUN
RUE D'HAUTEVILLE
RUE DE PARADIS
95
R. MARTEL
10
93
Château d'Eau
R. DES PET. ECURIES
RUE D'ENGHIEN
R. DE L'ÉCHIQUIER
RUE DU FAUBG POISSONNIÈRE
R. BLEUE
R. RICHER
BERGÈRE
TH. DU GYMNASE
BD DE STRASBOURG
RUE DU CHÂTEAU D'EAU
R. DE METZ
EL DORADO
STRASB-ST DENIS
BOULD BONNE NOUV.
BD ST DENIS
BD ST MARTIN
St Martin
Bne Nouv.
2
3
R. BEAUREGARD
R. D'ABOUKIR
R. DU CAIRE
89
96
90
91
94

Xe ARRONDISSt

Echelle

0 100 500

Métropolitain

Limite d'arrondisst
do de quartier

CARTES TA

154 Boulvd St Germ

THE BOBO ATTITUDE

Centre Commercial

2, rue de Marseille, Xe — Tel. +33 (0)1 42 02 26 08
and for children:
22, rue Yves-Toudic, Xe — Tel. +33 (0)1 42 06 23 81
www.centrecommercial.cc

Why go? I'm tempted to come here whenever I have a free moment. This brand is fast gaining ground. It began marketing to adults, and now children have their own address as well. Men will find an array of hipster chic options. There are super-cool styles for women here (rompers, anyone?), as well as trendy classic looks (*chapeaux* by famed hatter Larose).

The must-have A men's sweatshirt with the AMI, Alexandre Mattiussi label. Or how about the one with the flirty message "*Premier Baiser*" (First Kiss)? AMI has a boutique right next to mine on rue de Grenelle, so I think it deserves a little plug.

Say it like La Parisienne
"When are they going to open a store on the left bank?"

Asian Fashion

193, rue du Faubourg-Saint-Denis, X^e^
Tel. +33 (0)1 40 34 92 72
Another address for Indian clothing:
Sumangaly Tex
201, rue du Faubourg-Saint-Denis, X^e^
Tel. +33 (0)1 40 36 85 03

Why go? Let's say you've been invited to an Indian-themed costume party and have nothing to wear. This should be your destination. On the other hand, you can also shop here even if there's no such festivity in your future, because it's always good to have a sari in your closet.

→ **The must-have** A shimmering, richly colored sari. And costume jewelry bracelets that are perfect for summer beach wear or holiday parties.

Say it like La Parisienne

"I always wear a sari when I'm visiting Provence in the summertime. It's so practical."

Jamini

10, rue du Château-d'Eau, X^e^
Tel. +33 (0)9 82 34 78 53
and **10, rue Notre-Dame-de-Lorette, IXe**
Tel. +33 (0)9 83 65 62 22 — www.jaminidesign.com

90

Why go? This store is for those who are undaunted by the prospect of decorating with prints. It carries a vast selection of pillows, throws, and scarves that all make wonderful presents. The prints are produced in India by local artisans under the direction of Usha Bora. She's an Indian designer who's been living in France for the last fifteen years. The boutique got started in 2014 and has been so successful that they added another shop (10, rue Notre-Dame-de-Lorette, IXe).

→ **The must-have** Pretty little cosmetic containers. They make great gifts for all your friends.

Say it like La Parisienne

"Instead of getting new furniture, I change my cushions. It makes you feel like you've moved to a new home."

La Trésorerie/Café Smörgas

11, rue du Château-d'Eau, X^e^

Tel. +33 (0)1 40 40 20 46 — www.latresorerie.fr

Why go? It's a modern bazaar for all your household needs. Pillows, pots, plates, tablecloths, throws, dustpans, and even a shoeshine travel pack. It's not the most entertaining product line, but everything they carry is attractive.

The must-have I'm inclined to choose the cast-iron Swedish casserole—it looks very professional. But given my limited culinary abilities, I'll end up using it as a handsome display item.

Say it like La Parisienne

"Let's take a break at Smörgas, their Swedish café. They have great filter coffee."

Pop Market

50, rue Bichat, Xᵉ
Tel. +33 (0)9 52 79 96 86 — www.popmarket.fr

Why go? Your eyes may glaze over when you cross the threshold of this shop. But it's worth the effort if you're on a gift-buying mission. It's a mandatory pre-Christmas destination. You can snap up 70% of your holiday presents in a single place. Don't give up, and you'll ferret out pink flamingo paper clips and drumstick pens.

The must-have A toothbrush holder shaped like a fox. Sure, they also carry more serious items—the mini Bluetooth speaker, for instance.

Say it like La Parisienne
"How about a wall-mounted bear head bottle opener?"

Broc'Martel

12, rue Martel, Xe
Tel. +33 (0)1 48 24 53 43 — www.brocmartel.com

93

Why go? The place deserves a visit on its own merits. It's a *brocante*, a secondhand shop, but well organized. Owner Laurence Peyreade offers a carefully curated selection of items. When she discovers a rare treasure, she restores it before offering it for sale. 1950s furniture, fairground art, industrial objects, and loft-style lighting—they all seem to get along together very well.

→ **The must-have** If you're looking for vintage chairs, you'll often find sets of famous models here. I bought some for my garden.

Say it like La Parisienne

"It reminds me of the flea market, but even better."

Les Parigots

5, rue du Château-d'Eau, Xᵉ
Tel. +33 (0)1 42 00 22 26 — www.lesparigots.fr

Why go? As you've probably realized, I love anything reminiscent of an old-time Paris bistro. All it takes is a red-and-white checked napkin to capture my heart.

→ **What to order?** The *salade Républicaine* (mesclun, marinated salmon, organic cucumber, cherry tomatoes, and grapefruit) is royal.

Say it like La Parisienne

"It's so convenient that this place stays open until two o'clock in the morning."

Nanashi

31, rue du Paradis, Xe
Tel. +33 (0)1 40 22 05 55 — www.nanashi.fr

Why go? This is where the bobos go for bento boxes. You have three options: meat, fish, or vegetable. The décor is basic: wooden chairs, slate menus posted on the wall, and colorful lanterns—it's Japanese with a French accent. The cuisine is first and foremost healthy (at least the main courses are) but for a purely Japanese experience, you'll have to travel to Tokyo.

→ **What to order?** Any of the bento boxes.

Say it like La Parisienne

"Is fondant au chocolat *really Japanese?"*

les Vinaigriers

Les Vinaigriers

42, rue des Vinaigriers, X[e]
Tel. +33 (0)1 46 07 97 12 — www.lesvinaigriers.fr

Why go? I love the idea of a restaurant with the atmosphere of a country inn, and I'm a fan of simple wood bistro décor. Their motto "Seasonal products, home cooking" says it all. The food's delicious and the owners are charming.
→ **What to order?** The set menus are excellent value. The *gnocchis maison* are especially delicious.

Say it like La Parisienne
"I'd bet that Les Vinaigriers will soon be one of Boboland's most popular destinations."

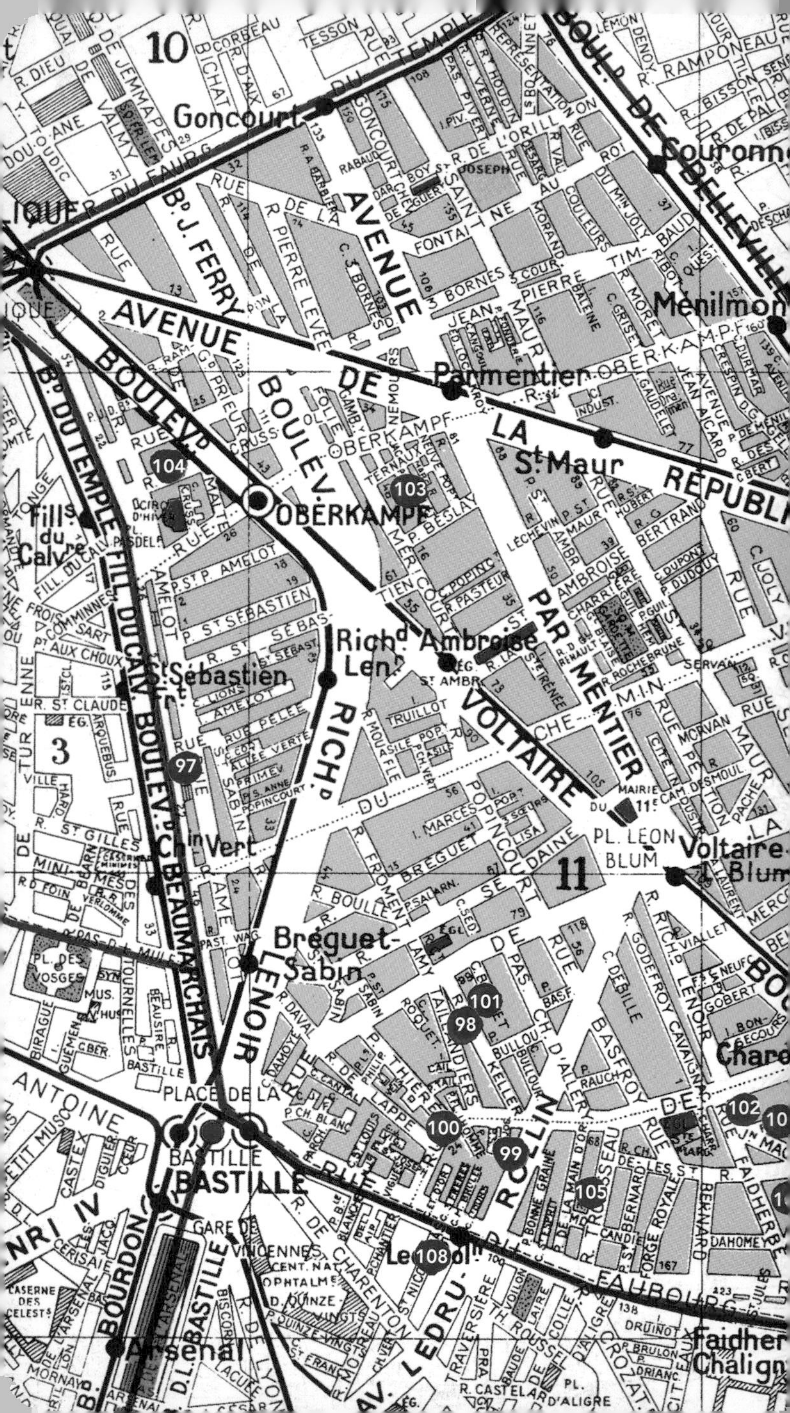

10
11
3
Goncourt
Ménilmon
Parmentier
St Maur
Oberkampf
Richd Lenr
St Ambroise
St Sébastien
Fills du Calvre
Chin Vert
Bréguet-Sabin
Voltaire
Bastille
Arsenal
Ledru-Rollin
Faidherbe Chaligny
Charonne
AVENUE PARMENTIER
AVENUE DE LA RÉPUBLIQUE
BOULEVARD VOLTAIRE
BOULEVARD RICHARD LENOIR
BOULEVARD DU TEMPLE
BOULEVARD BEAUMARCHAIS
BOULEVARD DE BELLEVILLE
Bd J. FERRY
RUE DU FAUBOURG ST ANTOINE
RUE OBERKAMPF
RUE ST MAUR
RUE DE LA ROQUETTE
RUE DE CHARONNE
RUE DE LAPPE
RUE AMELOT
RUE DE CHARENTON
AV. LEDRU-ROLLIN
PL. LÉON BLUM
PLACE DE LA BASTILLE
PL. DES VOSGES
MAIRIE DU 11e
GARE DE VINCENNES
104
103
97
98
99
100
101
102
105
108

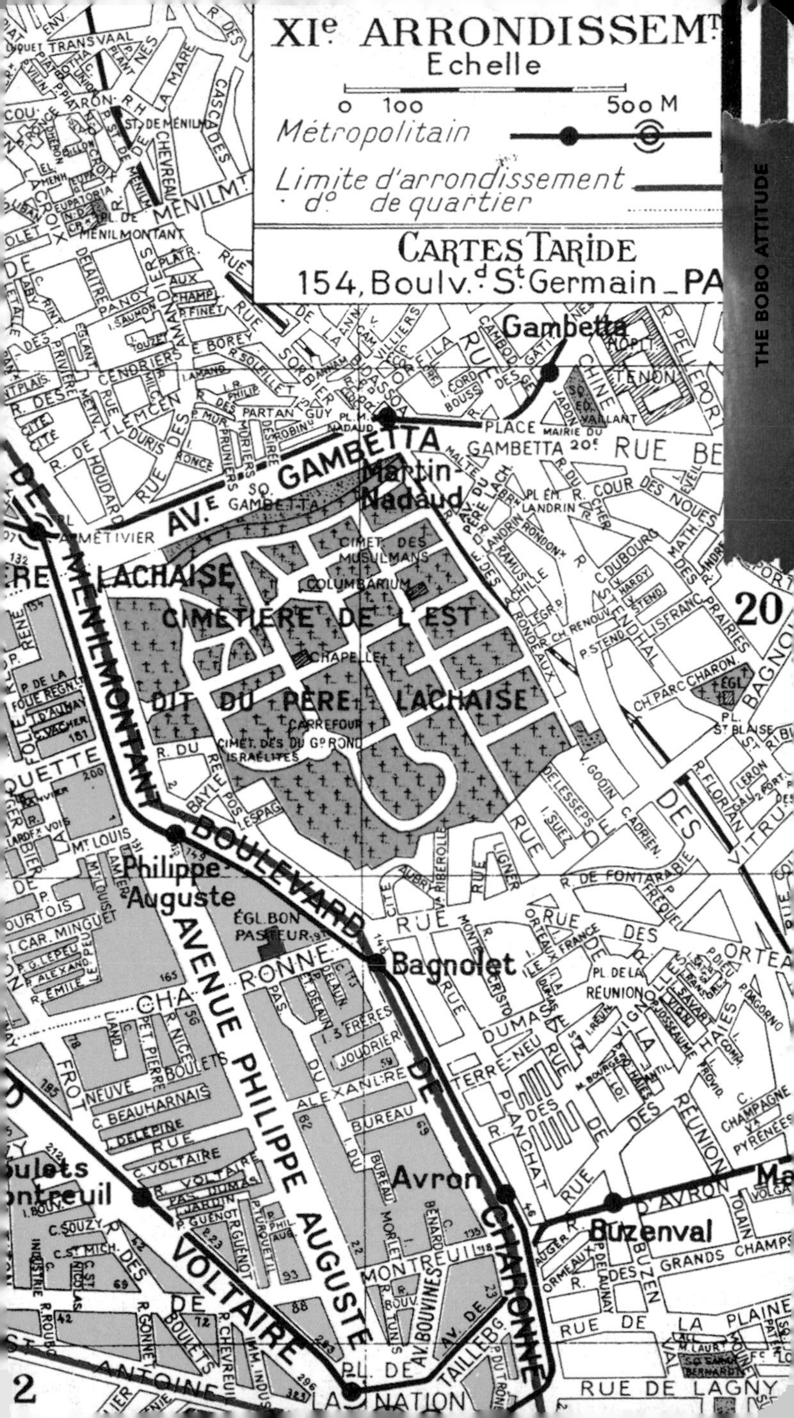

XIe ARRONDISSEMt
Echelle
0 100 500 M
Métropolitain
Limite d'arrondissement
d° de quartier
CARTES TARIDE
154, Boulv.d St Germain _ PA
THE BOBO ATTITUDE
Gambetta
PLACE GAMBETTA
MAIRIE DU 20E
AVE GAMBETTA
SQ. GAMBETTA
Martin-Nadaud
CIMET. DES MUSULMANS
COLUMBARIUM
CIMETIÈRE DE L'EST
CHAPELLE
DIT DU PÈRE LACHAISE
CARREFOUR
CIMET. DES ISRAÉLITES
DU GD ROND
MENILMONTANT
BOULEVARD
Philippe-Auguste
ÉGL. BON PASTEUR
Bagnolet
AVENUE PHILIPPE AUGUSTE
Avron
DE CHARONNE
Buzenval
VOLTAIRE
Boulets Montreuil
PL. DE LA NATION
RUE DE LAGNY
RUE DE LA PLAINE
RUE D'AVRON
GRANDS CHAMPS
RUE DES ORTEAUX
RUE DES VIGNOLES
RUE DE FONTARABIE
CH. PARC CHARONNE
PL. ST BLAISE
20

Khadi and Co

Khadi and Co.

82, blvd Beaumarchais, XIe
Tel. +33 (0)1 43 57 10 25 — www.khadiandco.com

Why go? To understand the significance of ethno-chic. It's one of my favorite places in Paris. The store stocks shawls, jackets, coats, blankets, tablecloths—you'll always find something irresistible. Everything here is of excellent quality and beautifully cut. The fabrics are ultra-comfortable, too. The *khadi*—a symbol established by Gandhi of the independence of those who "awoke to freedom," in Nehru's words, in the summer of 1947—demonstrates the remarkable expertise involved in hand-weaving this light, finely woven cloth.

The must-have If you can't decide, choose a scarf. You'll treasure it forever.

Say it like La Parisienne

"Bess Nielsen masterminds everything on display here. Scandinavian vitality (she's Danish) combined with Indian grace produces sensational designs."

AIMABLE
AIMABLE

Maison Aimable

16–18, rue des Taillandiers, XIe
Tel. +33 (0)9 82 53 16 18 — www.maison-aimable.com

Why go? This is the quintessential boutique for contemporary home décor. You'll want everything on display. It would be nice to have lunch sitting at that raw wood table topped with a pretty green plant. Vases, lamps, decorative objects—it's a sophisticated selection of articles sourced from everywhere, from Japan to the Netherlands.

The must-have An eggcup shaped like a chicken foot—if it's still in stock when you visit.

Say it like La Parisienne

"The owner is extremely aimable*—he's lovely."*

Les Fleurs

6, passage Josset, XIe

Tel. +33 (0)1 43 55 12 94 — www.boutiquelesfleurs.com

Why go? Gift shops are my obsession, and this one is a treasure. You'll find lovely items here, including wooden cards (yes, they're made of wood) printed with red pandas. You can either mail them or use them for decoration.

→ **The must-have** Nothing here is really essential, but ultimately everything is necessary. Like their children's lunch-box with a fox motif. You're sure to need it one of these days.

Say it like La Parisienne

"I'm going to get another notebook—I think I'm running low. And a little Liberty print suitcase; I don't think I have anything like it."

Urban Masala

2, passage Thiéré, XIe
Tel. +33 (0)1 55 28 57 68 — www.urban-masala.fr

Why go? Indians have their own version of contemporary design. The four founders of this boutique have created a savvy blend of tradition and modernity. Check it out—you'll understand once you've seen their bamboo stool.

The must-have The wall-mounted dish rack that's handmade using traditional artisanal techniques. It will add a touch of old Bombay to your kitchen décor.

Say it like La Parisienne
"I love sleeping under Indian duvet covers. It's like going on a romantic voyage while relaxing at home."

LouLou Addict

25, rue Keller, XIe
Tel. +33 (0)1 49 29 00 61 — www.loulouaddict.com

Why go? For so many reasons! For plastic boxes and paper or cloth napkins. Because you can never have enough containers. For decorated glasses and bowls. Even for oilcloth table covers. When you really need oilcloth, this is the place to go. I know—oilcloth can be hideous. All the more reason to keep this useful address handy.

The must-have The tableware, which is simple, just the way I like it.

Say it like La Parisienne

"I found that star-patterned oilcloth table cover here."

Carouche: Interprète d'Objets

18, rue Jean-Macé, XIe
Tel. +33 (0)1 43 73 53 03 — www.carouche.fr

Why go? Anyone who calls herself "an interpreter of objects" deserves our attention. Presenting a blend of restored secondhand furniture and contemporary items, Carouche specializes in furnishings from the 1950s and '60s. It's a well-stocked Ali Baba's cave—I could live in a setting like this.

The must-have All the American furniture—it's so different from French things. And how about a teapot decorated with painted flowers? It might be kitsch, but it brightens up tea time.

Say it like La Parisienne

"Did you see how she reinterpreted this lamp? She can put it back the way it was before if you don't like it."

Trolls et Puces/Belle Lurette

5, rue du Marché-Popincourt, XIe
Tel. +33 (0)1 43 14 60 00 (Trolls et Puces)
Tel. +33 (0)1 43 38 67 39 (Belle Lurette)
www.villagepopincourt.com

Why go? This is the secondhand boutique of your dreams. If you're into shabby chic, you'll be in heaven in this little neighborhood, where you'll also come across quite a few other dealers. It's a haven for bobos, but I should note that Trolls et Puces was established a lot earlier than most of the shops here. If you prowl around, you'll come across everything you need to reconstruct a 1940s movie set. I once found a fantastic looking vintage bag.

→ **The must-have** An enameled carafe or maybe a wicker-framed mirror. Ready, steady, rummage!

Say it like La Parisienne

"I love to go bargain-hunting here. There are a lot fewer people to compete against than on eBay."

Brugnon Miroiterie

134, rue Amelot, XIe
Tel. +33 (0)1 43 57 70 35 — www.brugnon-freres.fr

Why go? It's always good to have an address for mirrors and glass just in case something breaks. Or maybe you'll be overcome with a desire for insulated windows. This firm has been in business for over sixty years, so they have considerable experience. You can trust them. They'll provide you with free estimates and give you personalized advice.
The must-have I'm not sure there really are any must-haves in this type of shop. Maybe a window if you don't already have enough of them in your house.

Say it like La Parisienne

"I hang mirrors everywhere. I love bringing a touch of the Hall of Mirrors from Versailles to my own little hallway."

Kluger: Fabrique des Tartes

15, rue Trousseau, XIe
Tel. +33 (0)1 53 01 53 53 — www.tarteskluger.com

Why go? I love Catherine Kluger's story. The former copyright lawyer left it all behind to bake tarts. She's published acclaimed recipe books, too. Her values? Make them good, make them fresh, make them wholesome. I agree.

What to order? The only option is a tart. My favorite is a savory version featuring tomatoes and *chèvre*, seasoned with mint and basil. The chocolate one isn't too shabby either.

Say it like La Parisienne

"When I'm at the flea market, I stop by Kluger's Café Habitat (77, rue des Rosiers, Saint-Ouen) for a tart."

Restaurant/Bistro

Bistrot Paul Bert

18, rue Paul-Bert, XIe
Tel. +33 (0)1 43 72 24 01

Why go? It's the kind of French bistro I love (you've probably noticed I love a lot of them). The décor here is attractive and authentic—a zinc bar, tiled floors, waiters with a white towel tucked into their aprons, and a big mirrored wall. Classic home-style cooking, with something for everyone on the menu.

What to order? *Tartare de bœuf* and *baba au rhum*. Can someone point out the nearest gym?

Say it like La Parisienne

"I bring all my American friends here. It's exactly what they have in mind when they think of France."

Le Pure Café

14, rue Jean-Macé, XIe
Tel. +33 (0)1 43 71 47 22 — www.lepurecafe.fr

Why go? A traditional wooden bar is all it takes to make a place friendly and hospitable. It's thoroughly authentic—an ideal place to meet for an aperitif, especially during their Happy Hour.

→ **What to order?** The cured Wagyu beef platter. It appeals to my Japanese designer side. And it offers a change from the usual sliced sausage.

Say it like La Parisienne

"The perfect spot to shoot a movie that oozes with Parisian spirit."

Ines's all-time favorites

108 Caravane

A must for sofas

19 and 22 rue Saint-Nicolas, XIIe
Tel. +33 (0)1 53 02 96 96 (no. 19, La Maison)
Tel. +33 (0)1 53 17 18 55 (no. 22, La Table)
www.caravane.fr

Photo Credits
With sincere thanks to everyone who assisted in providing the images; photos courtesy of the locations except:

Céline Astorg p. 165
Patrice Bondurand p. 125
Yann Deret p. 98
Flammarion pp. 66, 72, 74 right, 96, 102, 132, 135, 136, 139, 142 top, 144, 145, 146 top left and bottom, 148–152, 166
Ines de la Fressange p. 14 top, 114
Ines de la Fressange and Sophie Gachet pp. 105 right, 106 left, 119 left, 171
Marianne Haas p. 30
Raphaël Hache p. 48
Hufton +Crow p. 58
Beata Komand p. 168
Guillaume de Laubier p. 52
Olivier Malingue p. 167
Dominique Maître p. 112
Pierre Monetta p. 104
Antoine Motard p.138
Amy Murrell p. 106 right
Pentagram p. 124
Kate Reiners pp. 23, 45, 65, 75, 89, 101, 118
Stone Paris p. 116
Grégoire Voevodsky p. 50

Notes

Notes

Notes

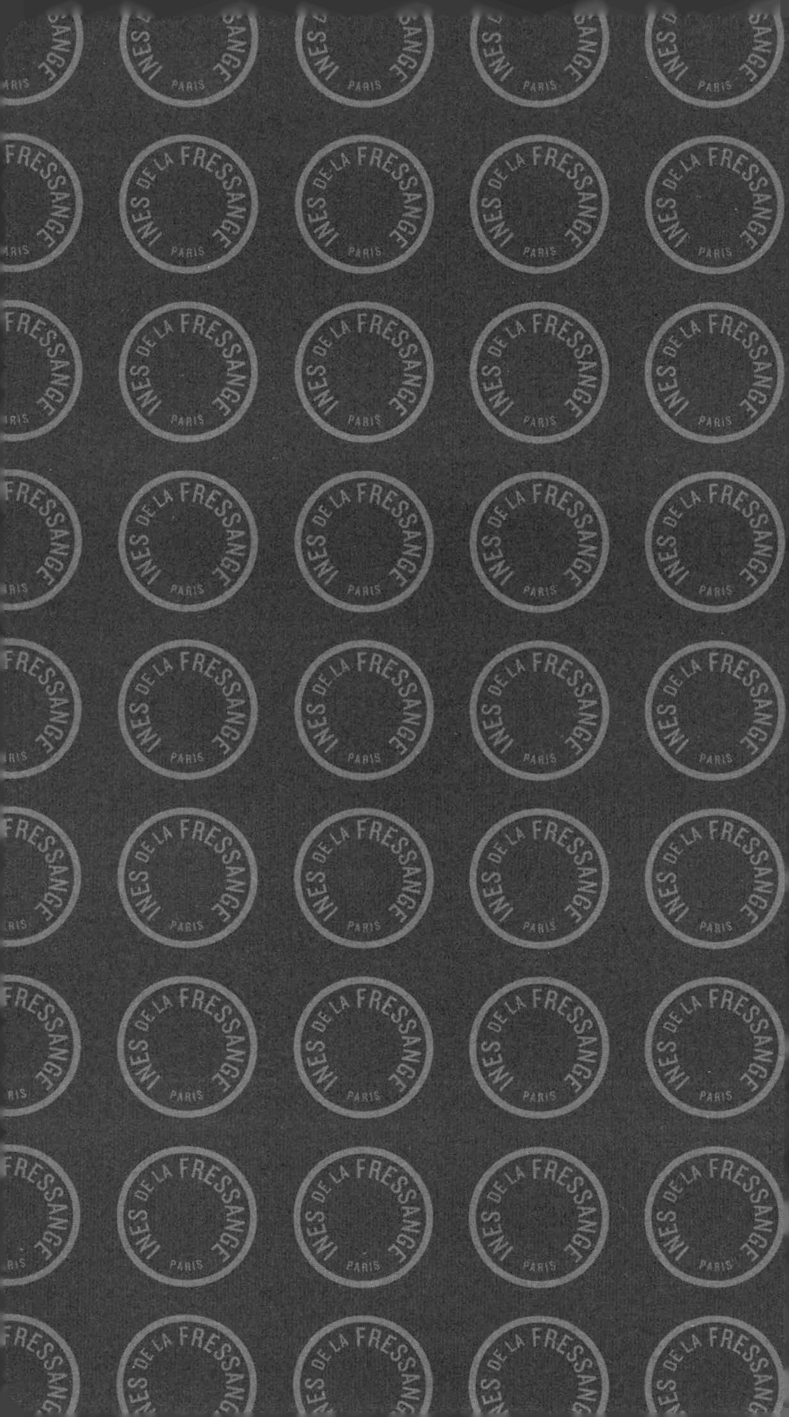
INES DE LA FRESSANGE
PARIS